FROM DAY TO DAY
A MESSAGE
FROM THE BIBLE
FOR EACH DAY
OF THE YEAR

FROM DAY TO DAY
A MESSAGE
FROM THE BIBLE
FOR EACH DAY
OF THE YEAR

by

Frank E. Gaebelein
Headmaster Emeritus, The Stony Brook School

A CANON PRESS BOOK

BAKER BOOK HOUSE
GRAND RAPIDS, MICHIGAN

To my children — Dorothy Laura Hampton,
Donn Medd Gaebelein, and Gretchen Elizabeth Hull
— who love the Lord and are walking in the truth

Acknowledgments

The following publishers have generously granted permission to use copyrighted material:

The American Bible Society, for portions of the *Today's English Version New Testament*. Copyright © American Bible Society 1966, 1971.

Darton, Longman & Todd, Ltd. and Doubleday and Company, Inc., for excerpts from *The Jerusalem Bible*, copyright © 1966.

Harper & Row Publishers, Inc., for passages from *Weymouth's New Testament in Modern Speech*.

The National Council of the Churches of Christ in the United States of America, for verses from the Revised Standard Version Bible.

The New York Bible Society International, for quotations from the *New International Version New Testament*.

Oxford University Press, for excerpts from *The New English Bible*. © The Delegates of the Oxford University Press and The Syndics of the Cambridge University Press 1961, 1970.

Thomas Nelson Inc., for use of the American Standard Version Bible, 1901.

Zondervan Publishing House, for permission to use the *Modern Language Bible-The New Berkeley Version in Modern English*. Copyright © 1945 59. 69

The Lockman Foundation, for permission to use portions of the New American Standard Bible, © 1960, 1962, 1963, 1968, 1971.

From *The New Testament in the Language of the People* by Charles W. Williams. Copyright 1966 by Edith S. Williams. Used by permission of Moody Press, Moody Bible Institute of Chicago.

PREFACE

As its title implies, this book has to do with daily Christian living. The messages that comprise it have been selected from thousands of comments I wrote in years past for *Our Hope, The Christian Observer,* and *The Presbyterian.* I have, however, so extensively revised and, in many cases, rewritten them as to make this a new book. The material it contains is completely different from that in *Looking Unto Him,* my other volume of daily meditations.

While these pages reflect my pilgrimage of many years spent in Christian education, writing, editorial work, and Bible teaching, they do this not through specific personal experiences but through sharing what I have learned from the Scriptures about serving God in the responsibilities of everyday life. So I have aimed in these brief comments on many texts to combine a measure of exposition with devotional and practical application of the Word of God. Always I have had in mind that the whole Bible bears witness to our Lord Jesus Christ, for while the New Testament speaks directly of Him, the lesser known as well as the familiar portions of the Old Testament also witness to Him in prophecy and other ways. As James Stewart says, "It was a favourite dictum of the preachers of a bygone day that, just as from every village in Britain there was a road which, linking on to other roads, would bring you to London at last, so from every text in the Bible, even the remotest and least likely, there was a road to Christ." The brief passages on which the messages collected in these pages are based come from all sixty-six books of the Bible. Many of the messages speak directly of Christ; others point by implication to His relation to all of life and service.

Essential to Christian discipleship is the daily discipline of Bible reading and prayer, particularly in these times when the voices of the mass media through the printed page and over the air are clamoring for our attention. It is my hope that this book may be an incentive for maintaining this discipline—not as a substitute for private prayer and reading of the Word but as an adjunct to them.

As for the order in which the Scripture portions and comments are arranged, I have sought a wide diversity. The needs of those who use a book of this kind are so varied and unpredictable that any set order might hamper flexibility in speaking to individual situations.

Most of the Scripture texts are from the King James Version, though a sizable number of them come from modern translations. Abbreviations for these follow this preface.

Finally, I desire to express my appreciation to the Canon Press for encouragement in the publication of this book and to Sue Peterson, Beth Lewis, and Carol Prester for their careful copy editing.

Arlington, Virginia

FRANK E. GAEBELEIN

Key to Abbreviations

BERKELEY	—The Modern Language Bible· The New Berkeley Version
JB	—The Jerusalem Bible
NASB	—The New American Standard Bible
NEB	—The New English Bible
NIV	—The New International Version
RSV	—The Revised Standard Version
TEV	—Today's English Version
WEYMOUTH	—The New Testament in Modern Speech, by Richard Francis Weymouth
WILLIAMS	—The New Testament in the Language of the People, by Charles B. Williams

JANUARY 1

And he that sat upon the throne said, Behold, I make all things new (REVELATION 21:5a).

The Bible recognizes the need for renewal more clearly than even the most idealistic of us. Moreover, it guarantees that this renewal will be accomplished. But in the attainment of change, the Bible is poles apart from man. Men see themselves as remaking the world by their own efforts; the Bible sees God, who enables Christians to be the salt of the earth, as doing this. And the Bible is right. What was told John on Patmos will ultimately be accomplished. He who occupies the throne of the universe promises, "Behold, I make all things new."

Then let us take heart and rejoice in this New Year. It will bring us closer to the time when the Lord Jesus Christ Himself will take control and, judgment having been executed and all things cleansed, there will be the new heaven and new earth in which righteousness and peace will remain forever. Meanwhile, ours is the daily responsibility to proclaim the Gospel of Christ and to work through the guidance of the Holy Spirit for needed change, till our Lord comes to consummate His kingdom.

JANUARY 2

Seek the Lord, and his strength: seek his face evermore (PSALM 105:4).

We seek the Lord because we need Him. We turn to Him for strength because we have no enduring strength of our own. As Paul wrote, "When we were yet without strength, in due time Christ died for the ungodly" (Romans 5:6).

The Lord's strength! To whom but the Lord Jesus can such a designation apply? He strengthens those enfeebled by sin. He shows us the face of His loving Father. Not only at the beginning of another year but throughout all its days we shall need to trust Him for strength. In prayer, in reading the Word, in serving others, we need constantly to seek His face. And as we do so, we shall find that His promise "Seek, and you shall find" (Luke 11:9) is completely true. "For the scripture says, 'Whoever believes in him will not be disappointed'" (Romans 10:11, TEV).

1

JANUARY 3

For he himself knew what he would do (JOHN 6:6).

"He knows his business." This is a colloquial way of characterizing a thoroughly competent person. Reverently we may think of it as expressing the sense of our text. For when the Lord Jesus asked Philip how bread might be secured for the hungry crowd, it was important for Him to test the faith of Philip—important not for Himself but for Philip's sake that he might have a lesson in the infinite resources of his Lord.

"He himself knew what he would do." This is always true of our Lord. There is comfort in the fact that He can never be taken by surprise. Though the circumstances of our lives sometimes seem planless, when they are in Christ's control we may be sure that our Lord knows what He is doing. To really trust such a Master means security from worry and concern. Therefore, it should result in better work. Christ indeed knows His business; ours is the responsibility of obeying His commands.

JANUARY 4

For by grace you have been saved through faith; and this is not your own doing, it is the gift of God—not because of works, lest any man should boast (EPHESIANS 2:8, 9, RSV).

What a wonderful declaration! Everything in it points to God and away from man. Grace, the unmerited favor of God, is the source of our salvation; faith is the channel, all is a gift. Twice in this sentence the least particle of human credit for salvation is repudiated in the words "not your own doing" and "not because of works." Even the verb with its passive voice ("you have been") speaks of God's saving activity in man's behalf. And with the phrase, "lest any man should boast," the absence of human effort in salvation is reiterated. In the light of all this, how grievous is the error that assigns to man any credit for his salvation!

But salvation is not only past but also present. Though we know that self-effort can never atone for sins of the past, somehow we are liable to think that we must help God save us here and now. If we could but realize more deeply that God has just one method of salvation in past, present, or future, and that His method is by grace through faith, we should be more ready to trust Him for our every need today.

JANUARY 5

Look to yourself, lest you too be tempted (GALATIANS 6:1b, RSV).

This is one of the things we are to do when someone falls into sin. If you will read the entire verse, you will see that we are called first of all to active helpfulness in behalf of the person who has fallen. "Restore him in a spirit of gentleness" is the next injunction. For it is not only the gesture of help that counts; all important is the spirit in which help is proffered. Here is where much of our efforts falls short. To offer aid to the sinner in a proud spirit is to rub salt into his wounds. Only one attitude, that of humility, may accompany our efforts to restore our brother or sister who has been overtaken in a fault. And the basis of that attitude lies in the honest recognition of our own human weakness and susceptibility to temptation.

JANUARY 6

Consider . . . Christ Jesus (HEBREWS 3:1).

Every one of us believers can look back and see how and when things would have been different had we but considered Christ Jesus. That time when sin gained the supremacy over us would never have occurred, had we been considering Him. But alas, we forgot Christ Jesus, and the enemy won the victory. Those hours of needless worry and concern would never have set us back, had we only heeded these words, "consider Christ Jesus."

Here is a simple prescription for spiritual living. The first thing on waking in the morning, do this: *Consider Christ Jesus.* Make it a rule to have your first conscious thoughts of Him. You can do it, for you are in charge of your own mind. Again, make it a rule to devote your last thoughts as you go to sleep to Him. This also you can learn to do. Thus your days will be bounded, so to speak, by consideration of the Lord Jesus. He will honor this effort to think of Him first and last; He will help you to keep Him in mind throughout the day.

JANUARY 7

And in nothing terrified by your adversaries (PHILIPPIANS 1:28a).

What inspiring words! If we only might have the faith to take them seriously! Observe exactly what Paul is saying. "In nothing," he writes, "terrified by your adversaries." Listen to it again, Christian: "In *nothing* terrified." Oh, how much you and I shall be delivered from, if we can but make Paul's attitude our own through the grace of God. Many of our difficulties are traceable to plain, downright fear. We are indeed making progress in Christian living when, like Paul, we refuse to be terrified by any adversaries at all.

JANUARY 8

If you chance to come upon a bird's nest, in any tree or on the ground, with young ones or eggs and the mother sitting upon the young or upon the eggs, you shall not take the mother with the young: you shall let the mother go, but the young you may take to yourself; that it may go well with you, and that you may live long (DEUTERONOMY 22:6,7, RSV).

As we glance through this chapter, together with the three that follow it, we see all kinds of relationships dealt with, ranging from marriage to the treatment of a bird's nest. Perhaps you are saying, "All very interesting; but what, after all, do these regulations have to do with us? We are under grace, not the law of Moses."

Well, this is what they have to do with us. They teach us that God is concerned with the whole of life. They show us that religion relates to everything we do. The Lord's claim upon us is a total one; He who said that not a sparrow falls to the ground apart from our Father's will, cares about our attitude toward His creation. From their beginning, our lives are lived in His sight, and in all our relationships, small or great, we are responsible to Him.

JANUARY 9

THE LORD THY GOD (Deuteronomy 28:58).

So the King James Version prints it. Moses calls it "this glorious and fearful name," and speaks of Israel's standing in awe of it. Let us ask ourselves a question about this greatest and most powerful of all names. We find it capitalized so that it may have all possible prominence and emphasis. Is it too naive to suggest that we look within our hearts to see whether the name is capitalized there? Surely not. It is one thing to read this holy name in capital letters in the pages of a book; it is quite another thing to write it large upon one's heart.

Yes, THE LORD THY GOD is a "jealous God" (Deuteronomy 5:8). He is a jealous God for our own good because He knows that our only hope of light and joy and peace and life comes from Himself, the only Lord God.

JANUARY 10

Remember them that are in bonds, as bound with them; and them which suffer adversity, as being yourselves also in the body (Hebrews 13:3).

If a man has a pain in some portion of his body, he is in no danger of forgetting it. Because the parts of his body are united, his nervous system keeps it before his consciousness. Such is the analogy of the latter part of this verse. We believers are to sympathize (literally, "suffer with") our fellow believers because they are organically united with us in the Church, which is our Lord's body. Similarly we are to remember those who are in bonds, considering that, as they are one body with us, we are bound with them.

There have been periods in the history of the Church when this injunction has been particularly needed. Such was the apostolic age; such too is our own time. In some places today Christians are in cruel hands. Throughout the world some believers are suffering persecution. And if God, purely of His grace and through no merit of our own, has left us free and unmolested, how can we forget the suffering members of that spiritual body to which Christ has united us? Surely it is not too much to ask that we remember them today before the Throne of Grace.

JANUARY 11

I will . . . make . . . the valley of Achor a door of hope
(HOSEA 2:15, RSV).

The valley of Achor had a dreadful history. It was the place
where the iniquitous Achan was stoned to death in the days of
Joshua (Joshua 7). The word means "trouble," and the very
sound of its syllables is dolorous. But here in this prophecy of
Hosea, which so scathingly denounces the unfaithfulness of
Israel as spiritual adultery, Jehovah promises that for erring
Israel He will turn the valley of Achor into a "door of hope."
And that is exactly what our God is always doing for His children. The darkest places in our lives can become, in His overruling providence, the doors of hope. The very depths of sin
finally bring the prodigal to his senses as God opens the door of
salvation. Let us not forget that our great God knows how to
sanctify to us our deepest distress.

JANUARY 12

*And the king said again unto Esther on the second day at
the banquet of wine, What is thy petition, queen Esther?
and it shall be granted thee: and what is thy request? and
it shall be performed, even to the half of the kingdom*
(ESTHER 7:2).

Esther has found favor with Ahasuerus; the king has held out
to her his golden scepter. Mordecai has been exalted and Haman compelled to honor him. Now the king and Haman come
to Esther's banquet. It was the custom of oriental monarchs at
a banquet such as this to show the greatest liberality to their
favorites. And these words of Ahasuerus to Esther are fully in
accord with this custom.

But let us look at this scene as a picture of a prerogative that
is the birthright of every Christian. We who know the Lord
Jesus Christ as Saviour have the right to come at any time into
God's presence bringing our petitions. Every time Esther went
unbidden before Ahasuerus, her life was in jeopardy; a sudden
change of mood on the king's part could lead to her downfall.
But our God does not vacillate. With Him there is "no variable-
ness, neither shadow of turning" (James 1:17). Because of the
work of Christ, our right of access to the heavenly throne is continuous and unrestricted. Are you using that right daily, and,
like Esther, are you using it in behalf of others?

JANUARY 13

Therefore turn thou to thy God; keep mercy and judgment, and wait on thy God continually (HOSEA 12:7).

It is all very well to talk about turning to the Lord. Words of repentance sometimes come cheap. But the kind of turning to God that counts rests upon more than oral testimony. Said a Christian lawyer when told of the large and enthusiastic testimony meetings conducted in a certain church, "For a legally trained mind there is a vast difference between testimony and evidence." There is indeed a difference, and it applies not only to public worship but also to every part of the Christian life. Repentance must be backed by positive evidence. Hosea makes this very plain. "'Therefore," he insists, "turn thou to thy God." That is the call to repentance. "Keep mercy and judgment, and wait on thy God continually." That is the call to corroboration of repentance. The penitent who goes on to manifest in his life godly qualities like mercy and justice and who trusts God continually is substantiating his change of heart by evidence no one can gainsay.

JANUARY 14

For thou art my lamp, O Lord: and the Lord will lighten my darkness (2 SAMUEL 22:29).

In the great song of deliverance occupying this entire chapter David did not ask God to be his Lamp and lighten his darkness. No, David knew that the Lord, who had been his Lamp in the past, would never fail to lighten his darkness in the future. Therefore he could say of Him, "The Lord will lighten my darkness."

We Christians may have the certainty of David. As believers we may know that the Lord is our Lamp, for He who is the Light of the world dwells in our hearts by faith. We may be sure, therefore, that Christ Himself will lighten our darkness. Though clouds thicken till the darkness may be felt, nevertheless no shadow is so impenetrable that the Light of the world cannot dispel it. Yes, the world is dark. But Christ is the true Light. And so our need is not just for spiritual illumination. God has provided that in full measure. Our need is rather the practical one of walking in the light as He is in the light.

JANUARY 15

Death and life are in the power of the tongue (PROVERBS 18:21a).

This fact cannot be too much stressed among Christian people. Many a reputation has been killed, many a good name murdered, by a careless tongue. But, thank God, the proverb is not merely negative. Life is also in the power of the tongue. Oh, what blessing there would be if all the readers of these words would resolve today to see how much good they might do with their tongues! From the simple word of kindness, the phrase of appreciative good will, to the sincere witness for Christ—what a wealth of opportunity for good! Let us resolve today to make our tongues instruments of healing and life.

JANUARY 16

But they held their peace, and answered him not a word; for the king's commandment was, saying, Answer him not (ISAIAH 36:21).

Chapters thirty-six, thirty-seven, and thirty-eight of Isaiah are unique. They present an historical interlude, placed here in the center of the greatest of the Old Testament prophets, which is almost exactly duplicated in one other place (2 Kings 18–20) and related in part still elsewhere (2 Chronicles 32, 33). It is a rare instance of a thrice-repeated incident in the Old Testament. This is the narrative of the Assyrian ultimatum delivered by the insulting Rabshakeh. It tells about King Hezekiah's reliance upon the Lord through Isaiah's advice and shows how the Lord delivered the Israelites, followed by how He healed Hezekiah.

The insults of the Rabshakeh had reached their height. "But," the record says, "they held their peace, and answered him not a word, for the king's commandment was, saying, Answer him not." What an illustration of the power of quiet and self-restraint even in the face of the most wicked abuse! These men of Judah kept silent. It must have been an effort for them to do it, but they held their tongues. Why? Well, they held their tongues because the king had said, "Answer him not." We too need to learn to be quiet. When the tempter besieges our souls, there is no stronger defense than the quietness of a heart that relies on Christ.

JANUARY 17

Then the king said unto me, For what dost thou make request? So I prayed to the God of heaven (NEHEMIAH 2:4).

It was not an audible prayer Nehemiah made. He was in the presence of the great King Artaxerxes. Much depended on the king's reply. But Nehemiah did not answer before lifting up his heart to God in a silent yet definite prayer for help. The book bearing the name of this man of God shows that continual prayerfulness of mind was one of his great characteristics. It is also a characteristic every Christian may cultivate—this looking to God in silent prayer before every decision, after every blessing, all through the day. For to do this is really to practice the presence of God.

JANUARY 18

The burden of Moab (ISAIAH 15:1a).

Who were the Moabites? Genesis 19:37 tells us that they were descendants of Lot. Their ancestor was halfhearted in allegiance to God, but they went all the way into heathenism. Through the years they were the enemies of God's people, turning against them and conquering them in the period of the judges and then being conquered by Israel. Later they revolted and were again subjected under David. So it went. Their record is one long story of opposition to the chosen people; their doom was deserved.

But there is a gleam of light upon this depressing record of Moab. Recall the book of Ruth. Its heroine was a Moabitess. This young woman, so notable for her loving fidelity, was of that despised stock. Yet think what the grace of God did through her. To her was given a place in the Messianic line; the ancestress of David, she has her own mention in the genealogy of our Saviour (Matthew 1:5). So Ruth, the Moabitess, reminds us that no one is beyond God's saving grace. The Bible never makes the mistake, to which human judgment is so prone, of condemning people en masse. Isaiah was right in predicting doom upon Moab. Yet God could take Ruth from this corrupt people and by His grace make her one of the most blameless characters in Scripture.

JANUARY 19

Speaking the truth in love (EPHESIANS 4:15).

It is not enough for Christians to speak the truth. That is taken for granted. Many a sensitive personality, however, has been cruelly hurt by the truth blurted out in an uncharitable and unfeeling way. So Christians are to speak the truth in love. That requires spiritual tact; it demands nothing less than the guidance of the Holy Spirit. And there are occasions when it also takes high courage. Sometimes the raw truth can cause great pain. Then it needs to be mixed with compassionate love. Lord, teach us how to speak the truth in love!

JANUARY 20

And Moses returned unto the Lord, and said, Lord, wherefore hast thou so evil entreated this people? why is it that thou hast sent me? For since I came to Pharaoh to speak in thy name, he hath done evil to this people; neither hast thou delivered thy people at all (EXODUS 5:22, 23).

To act immediately is not the rule of God's dealing with His people. Moses' and Aaron's demand that Pharaoh let the Israelites go out of Egypt met summary rejection. The number of bricks the people were required to make was increased, and the straw necessary for making the bricks was withheld. What had seemed hope of speedy deliverance had apparently been turned into grave calamity. But it was all part of God's plan. Moses was meeting the essential test of endurance and patience.

There are times when blessing is withheld, and we meet difficulty and disappointment. For occasionally there come parentheses of testing in God's dealings with His children. In such situations we need to trust when we cannot understand. God will not fail us. As He brought Moses and Israel out of Egypt, so He will deliver us in His good time.

JANUARY 21

Let not the sun go down upon your wrath (EPHESIANS 4:26).

This is one of the lesser known commands of the New Testament. Yet what a wise and practical principle it sets before us! Applied in the home it averts contention and heartbreak, used among friends it prevents severance of bonds of love, in churches it obviates disunity, and applied in society it would go far to avoid strife. It is a sovereign cure for many evils that beset human relationships because it is an expression of Christ's great commandment of love. If we have never before taken it in earnest, or if we have forgotten it, let us practice it today.

JANUARY 22

The valley of vision (ISAIAH 22:1a).

"The valley of vision." Ordinarily one would expect such a word as "mountain" or "hill" to be used with "vision," the natural thing being to imagine a vision in connection with a height. But Isaiah says, "the valley of vision," and in doing so is closer to reality than if he had used the more obvious figure. After all, it is in the valleys rather than upon the high places of our lives that we have our greatest visions of God. We are so constituted that, when exalted, we tend to be self-sufficient, and a self-sufficient man never has a great vision of the Almighty. But when we are in the valleys—oppressed, needy, perplexed, or sorrowful—then we reach out to God, and then He reveals Himself.

Job, who had one of the greatest visions of God, went down into the valley more deeply than any man but Christ. Ezekiel was in the valley of the Babylonian captivity when he had the stupendous vision of God and the throne amid the flashing wheels, the swiftly-flying, living creatures, and the terrible crystal. Paul was in dire straits, when he was caught up into the third heaven and heard things unspeakable, not lawful for man to utter. John was in the valley of exile on Patmos when he saw the heavens opened and the future conquests of Christ unveiled before his dazzled eyes. So when you and I are in the valley, let us look up; God is able to give us also, in accordance with our needs, strengthening and comforting visions of Himself.

JANUARY 23

Prove all things (1 Thessalonians 5:21a).

In other words, we Christians are to be properly skeptical. We are not to accept everything at its face value, for Satan is a liar who disguises himself as an angel of light. He is a wily adversary and a master of spiritual camouflage. He even knows how to cloak denial of the faith with Scripture and how to mask sin with seeming virtue. Proving, however, implies a standard. For us that standard is the Word of God, which in its application to every moral and spiritual question is never out of date. Let us be like the Berean Christians (Acts 17) who searched the Scriptures daily to prove whether what was taught them was so.

JANUARY 24

And whatsoever mine eyes desired I kept not from them, I withheld not my heart from my joy. . . . Then I looked on all the works . . . and, behold, all was vanity and vexation of spirit, and there was no profit under the sun. . . . Therefore I hated life (Ecclesiastes 2:10, 11, 17).

"Whatsoever mine eyes desired I kept not from them, I withheld not my heart from any joy." This repudiation of any check on personal desire is attractive to our human nature. But it leads to boredom, and boredom leads to cynicism. No wonder the Preacher's license in following every desire of his heart culminated in the despairing cry, "Behold, all was vanity and vexation of spirit."

Once a man begins to see life as futile and existence as profitless, he does not stop there. That which has no meaning for the human spirit turns into an object of loathing. So the Preacher reached bottom in these four words: "Therefore, I hated life." What a warning for a time such as this! Education is necessary, but it can never by itself give peace of heart to a restless soul. Nor can pleasure, pursued to the end, no matter on how lavish a level—even to that of a Solomon—bring anything but cynical hatred of life.

The Preacher said, "I hated life"; but Christ said, "I am come that they might have life, and that they might have it more abundantly" (John 10:10).

JANUARY 25

And what I say unto you I say unto all, Watch (MARK 13:37).

Have you ever thought of watching as an evidence of your love for your Lord? A dear one is absent from home. The day of his return draws near. The hour is almost at hand. How eagerly those who are waiting watch for the first sight of the well-loved form and the first sound of the cherished voice.

We Christians claim the Lord Jesus as the supreme object of our love. He is not with us in physical presence, but some day He will return. Are we watching for Him? Do we want to see His face and hear His voice? Do we love Christ enough to look for Him daily?

JANUARY 26

Examine yourselves, whether ye be in the faith (2 CORINTHIANS 13:5a).

It is a wholesome thing for a Christian to do what Paul advised the Corinthian believers to do. Self-examination, provided that it aims to discover whether a Christian is in the faith, is a valuable aid to spiritual growth. When Paul urged his readers to ascertain whether they were in the faith, he certainly meant that they were to do more than go over the creed in order to find out whether they assented to the Gospel. Knowing something of his dealings with the church at Corinth, we have every good reason to believe that for Paul to "be in the faith" meant that he lived in the faith and that the faith lived in him. Paul's epistles are noteworthy for their practical emphasis. He never left the faith hanging in thin air as a purely intellectual proposition, but insisted on its practical implications. Being "in the faith" was his way of stating Christ's command, "Abide in me" (John 15:4). Let us take these words of Paul as a challenge to examine ourselves today, aiming to discover not only whether we are orthodox in creed but also whether we are really living "in the faith."

JANUARY 27

I poured out my complaint before him; I shewed before him my trouble (PSALM 142:2).

To whom do we tell our troubles? Suppose that something very distressing occurs to us today. What will our first impulse be? Will it be to go to our husband or wife, father, mother, or friend and pour out the trouble? This is very human and there is nothing intrinsically wrong with it. But we have a higher confidant. First of all, we should pour out our complaints before Jesus, our divine Friend. Before we tell either relative or friend our distress, we should share it with the Lord. It may also be wise to go on to discuss the matter with some dear one. Yet taking the Lord Jesus into our confidence will often give such quietness that the trouble need not be passed on to distress a single other person.

JANUARY 28

For there they that carried us away captive required of us a song (PSALM 137:3).

This is the most nostalgic of the psalms; its first half-dozen verses are a poignant expression of homesickness. It is the song of the captives in Babylon, but by that universality so characteristic of the inspired Word it speaks for us also. In it are voiced the feelings, not only of the captive Jews, but also of Christians who realize that they are sojourners and strangers in this present world.

How callous those Babylonian captors were! They insisted that the Jews, homesick and sad at heart, entertain them with songs. And the world is still out of sympathy with the children of God. Yet we believers also have a song; with David we may say of the Lord, "He hath put a new song in my mouth, even praise unto our God" (Psalm 40:3). But though the world may not ask for it, nevertheless it is necessary for us to sing it. For, as David goes on to say, "Many shall see it, and fear, and shall trust in the Lord" (Psalm 40:3).

"What," some one says, "*see* a song?" Yes, that is correct, because there is such a thing as singing with your life. The Christian who walks consistently and happily with God is living a "song" attractive enough to lead some who see it to trust in the Lord.

JANUARY 29

Hold fast that which is good (1 THESSALONIANS 5:21b).

Obviously there is little point in this advice unless there is danger of losing what is good. One does not exhort a person to hold onto something that may not be lost. And it is decidedly possible to lose the good. Consider the matter of character, for instance. Through succumbing to temptation a Christian may fail to hold fast to character and so lose it. The eternal security of the believer is a great truth, but it may be misapplied. It certainly does not mean that the virtues we have are incapable of being lost. We may lose our reputation and purity, our love for others, our honesty, and ultimately our reward. Yes, we need to hold fast what is good, for none of us has the privilege of taking his character for granted.

JANUARY 30

I know that the Lord will maintain the cause of the afflicted, and the right of the poor (PSALM 150:12).

There is never any doubt as to which side the Lord is on; when it comes to matters of justice, God is always for the afflicted and underprivileged. The strange thing, however, is that some of us who are God's people are not always on the same side as the Lord. Somehow the plight of the afflicted and the rights of the poor touch us all too little. In certain cases the doctrine of the return of Christ may be so misapplied as to foster unconcern regarding the needs of present sufferers. The fault is not with the blessed hope but with our hearts. We are never to minimize the hope of our Lord's coming, but we never should make it an excuse to avoid the duty of ministering *now* to the afflicted. The same Apostle John, who begins the third chapter of his epistle with a beautiful statement of the return of Christ (1 John 3:1-3), goes on in that very chapter to say: "But if anyone has this world's goods and sees his brother in need, yet closes his heart against him, how does God's love dwell in him?" (1 John 3:17, RSV).

JANUARY 31

All we like sheep have gone astray; we have turned every one to his own way; and the Lord hath laid on him the iniquity of us all (ISAIAH 53:6).

In this central verse of Isaiah's fifty-third chapter we have one of the great universal statements in Scripture. What it says holds true not just for the majority of humanity; nor does it apply only to ninety percent of them. No, it applies to all of us. The whole human race is included, with the exception of Jesus the Son of God, who, though He was truly man, never sinned. Isaiah was not at this point confessing the sins of Israel alone; this was a greater and wider confession. For it is a fact that "all we like sheep have gone astray." Every human being must join in the lament, "we have turned everyone to his own way."

But this wonderful sentence contains another clause. And that clause gives us the remedy for the universal transgression of humanity. "The Lord," continues Isaiah, "hath laid on him the iniquity of us all." In keeping with the rest of this profound chapter, it is plain that by "him" the prophet means the Messiah. For Christ was different from all other men. Born of the virgin (Isaiah 7:14; Matthew 1:23; Luke 1:26-34), He was not only man but God. As the God-Man, He alone was free from sin. Of all who ever lived, He never strayed from the will of God. He was the perfect offering for sin, and on His thorn-crowned head God placed the iniquity of a lost race.

That is the Gospel. May we never get beyond an attitude of humble gratitude for the grace of our Saviour in taking upon Himself the iniquity of us all.

FEBRUARY 1

*Is there anything whereof it may be said, See, this is new?
it hath been already of old time, which was before us*
(ECCLESIASTES 1:10).

The Preacher had seen all he wished to see, learned all he
wanted to learn, had all he desired, and still was not happy.
Having departed from his early devotion to the Lord, he des-
cended into a cynicism that found all of life vain and futile.
"Is there anything really new, fresh, and unspoiled?" That is
what the Preacher was asking. And how few are the things
that are really new! Much we call new is mere novelty. Origi-
nality in any field, whether in literature, art, or science, is one
of the rarest of achievements, so rare that some even doubt its
possibility. Nevertheless, there is one realm where the new
finds daily embodiment. When the Lord Jesus instructed Nico-
demus, he was giving teaching that was really new. For a person to be born again is not a repetition of any prior experience.
Paul did not exaggerate when he said of regeneration, "If any
man be in Christ, he is a new creature: old things are passed
away; behold, all things are become new" (2 Corinthians 5:17).

Christ is the great Renewer. Everyone who has been changed
by Him into a new creation is a living reply to cynicism and
frustration. Has He made you new, and are you being renewed
in Him day by day?

FEBRUARY 2

With my soul have I desired thee in the night (ISAIAH
26:9a).

Some of God's choice gifts are unrecognized. For example,
the times when sleep fails may bring great blessing of soul if
used aright. Isaiah knew what to do with them. "With my soul,"
he said, "have I desired thee in the night." We may indeed
spend time in intercessory prayer if sleep does not come. But
intercession, important though it is, is not the only kind of soul
exercise. Surely it pleases God to hear us say we love Him. It
would be a strange relationship of a child to his father that con-
sisted only of pleas for aid for self and others. Human parents
know the joy of hearing a child freely express its love. So must
it be with God and us. In the quiet of the night, let us tell God
that our hearts desire Him; faltering though our words are, let
us express our love for Him who first loved us.

FEBRUARY 3

How hard it is for them that trust in riches to enter into the kingdom of God (MARK 10:24b).

Here the Lord Jesus explains why the possession of riches can lead to disqualification from entrance into the kingdom of God. It is not just the riches; it is trusting in them that is the hindrance. Trust is essential for entrance into the kingdom, but it must have the right object. Centered in anything except God it is a fatal obstacle to acceptance by Him.

You may not be trusting in riches, because you do not possess them. That is hardly to your credit. The question is, Would you trust in riches if you had them? And if you do not have wealth to trust in, are you relying on some other thing, whether good name, personality, learning, family background, or good deeds? Only those who are trusting in Christ alone can enter the kingdom of heaven.

FEBRUARY 4

And it shall be well with thee (PSALM 128:2b).

This is the psalm of family life, beautifully descriptive of a godly home. The words "blessed," "bless," and "happy" are prominent. Yet the word "fear" occurs twice in its six verses. There is no conflict here. The first verse sounds the keynote, as it declares, "Blessed is every one that feareth the Lord." Then comes a picture of the God-fearing man with his loving wife and children, after which the certainty of his blessing is repeated. "Behold," (the word is like a finger pointing out the scene) "that thus shall the man be blessed that feareth the Lord" (v. 4).

All this is simple and at the same time important. Though this psalm cannot be dated with any great accuracy, it probably was written about twenty-four or twenty-five hundred years ago. Yet in all that time the biblical criterion for happiness has not changed. Only the home based upon that reverential respect for God which the Old Testament calls "the fear of the Lord" can attain the kind of happiness described in these half-dozen verses. If the pattern of married life today so often differs from the beautiful tranquillity portrayed in this gem of Hebrew poetry, it may well be because of the preoccupation with purely secular and materialistic values that leaves little place for the fear of the Lord.

FEBRUARY 5

And Levi made him a great feast in his own house: and there was a great company of publicans and of others that sat down with them (LUKE 5:29).

This act upon the part of Levi (Matthew) took place immediately after he began to follow the Lord Jesus. He went home and arranged a great social gathering for a very particular purpose; he wanted to introduce his friends to Jesus.

Christian friend, have you ever done that? Have you ever used your home for the purpose of introducing to your Lord those who are strangers to Him? Rightly considered, that should be a function of every Christian home. The Lord's presence and Spirit should be so apparent in it and its occupants as to introduce those who come there to Jesus.

FEBRUARY 6

The Lord weigheth the spirits (PROVERBS 16:2b).

Only God can weigh the imponderable. No man can perfectly weigh the spirit of another man, for no human scale is adequate for such a measurement.

How does God weigh the spirits? The process is inscrutable to the human mind. Because God alone is omniscient, He only can see deeply enough to observe all the facts on which His justice is based. Because He only is perfect in His wisdom, He alone can make perfect decisions. And because He alone is absolutely just, His decisions will always be right. Yet though we cannot understand the process of divine justice, we may be fully assured of the result. When the Lord weighs the spirits, there cannot be even a hair's breadth deviation from perfect justice.

Meditation on this fact shows us our need of Christ. The contemplation of God's heavenly balances brings us to the only One perfect enough to meet the searching test of divine justice.

FEBRUARY 7

Whosoever will, let him take the water of life freely (REVELATION 22:17b).

"Whosoever." What a great word that is! It is God's own invitation, inviting everybody everywhere to drink of the life-giving water. "Whosoever." There was a time when we did not trust Christ. And when we did enter into salvation, it was only through the portals of that precious word "whosoever." It is God's great missionary word. With it ringing in our ears, how dare we restrict the offer of salvation to any country or people or race? "Whosoever." Not by chance does it appear in the closing chapter of God's Book, for it shows His purpose from the beginning to the end of His written revelation. Christ used it, the apostles preached it, every Christian must pass it on. Is it in your vocabulary in a practical way, so that by the witness of your life, by your gifts, and by the words of your mouth you too are inviting lost men and women to come to Christ?

FEBRUARY 8

And we will not forsake the house of our God (NEHEMIAH 10:39b).

"We will not forsake the house of our God." This noble resolve is one we need today. All about us are those who have actually forsaken the house of their God. Nurtured in Christian homes and churches, they have gone out to found their own homes. But in many cases those homes are secular and godless. If there is a lack of spiritual power and moral leadership, one of the reasons is the widespread neglect of the public worship of God. The author of Hebrews warns against "forsaking the assembling of ourselves together" (Hebrews 10:25). Unless the excuse is that of illness or some other emergency, no Christian within reach of a church where the Gospel is preached has any right to forsake the worship of God on the Lord's Day. Nor may parents expect their children to grow in grace, unless they themselves faithfully attend the house of God. Let us pray for revival. But let us remember that we cannot expect revival to come to people who on the Lord's day are turning their backs on God.

FEBRUARY 9

The Lord shall guide thee continually (ISAIAH 58:11a).

The adverb "continually" adds an important shade of meaning. There are times when we are perfectly sure that God is guiding us; things go so beautifully, events dovetail so providentially, that we do not have the least doubt of the Lord's leading. But there are other times when we wonder whether He is guiding us at all. Plans miscarry and difficulties multiply, even though we seek earnestly to do God's will. Yet if we are His, if we are wholly committed to Christ Jesus, we may trust His leading in dark times as well as light. It makes no difference whatever the direction of our path is, or whether or not we are conscious of God's guidance. The divine Word promises, "The Lord shall guide thee continually." And when God promises to do a thing continually, He does it all the time. So long as we are fully committed to our Lord, we may rely on His constant leading.

FEBRUARY 10

And when they had lifted up their eyes, they saw no man, save Jesus only (MATTHEW 17:8).

The disciples could not remain gazing indefinitely at the transfiguration. That was Peter's wish, expressed in his thoughtless suggestion about the three tabernacles. No, Peter, James, and John had to leave the mount and descend to their daily life. God could have sent Moses and Elijah down with them to help in their ministry. Instead He simply showed them Jesus only, after the glory of the transfiguration had passed.

So we are reminded that, if we have Jesus, we have all. It has not been God's purpose to reveal Moses and Elijah directly to us, nor has He been transfigured before our eyes. But He has given us the Lord Jesus. And Jesus is enough. Having Him we have everything; lacking Him, we have nothing of eternal value.

FEBRUARY 11

I was in prison, and ye came unto me (MATTHEW 25:36b).

There is a sense in which respectability hinders real Christianity. Some persons are religious snobs; they feel that the Lord is present only in beautiful churches and refined surroundings. But all the time He is also outside—on the street corners, in the slums, or within the prisons. Wherever there is human need, wherever there are sinners, there the Lord Jesus is. Seek Him in places set apart to Him, yes; but if you would learn more about His tender love, learn also to know Him in ministering to the poor and oppressed, the hungry and the afflicted.

FEBRUARY 12

And this is his name whereby he shall be called, THE LORD OUR RIGHTEOUSNESS (JEREMIAH 23:6b).

"THE LORD OUR RIGHTEOUSNESS," in Hebrew "Jehovah-tsidkenu," is one of the Old Testament names of our Saviour. How closely interwoven it is with our redemption! Because we are by nature unrighteous, we need "Jehovah-tsidkenu." What we do not possess in ourselves, and never can possess by self-effort, He gives us freely. It is of the very essence of Gospel truth that Christ clothes the sinner with His own perfect righteousness. Apart from this gracious act of placing upon the sinner Christ's spotless righteousness, there is no salvation. Human righteousness, no matter how exalted, is not good enough for God. He demands perfection. "Be ye therefore perfect, even as your Father which is in heaven is perfect" (Matthew 5:48). But we are imperfect, and we know it. We are sinful, and confess it. And then we look in faith to the cross and lay our sins on Jesus, "the spotless Lamb of God." When we do that, trusting Him fully, His righteousness becomes ours, and He is our "Jehovah-tsidkenu."

FEBRUARY 13

I hold you in my heart. . . . *For God is my witness, how I yearn for you all with the affection of Christ Jesus* (PHILIPPIANS 1:7, 8, RSV).

Between Paul and the Philippians there were close bonds of love and understanding. Probably no man in Christian history bore heavier burdens than Paul. Yet he was not too busy to carry in his heart a host of Christians, not only at Philippi but in all the churches. "I have you in my heart . . . how greatly I long after you all with the affection of Jesus Christ," he said.

Our spiritual responsibilities are but a fraction of Paul's. Yet every Christian is responsible for some others. We are all in a kind of pastoral relationship to other persons. Parents are responsible for children, brothers for brothers, friends for friends. Are we accepting these responsibilities as Paul accepted his? Are there those of whom we may truly affirm in respect to their souls' welfare, "I have you in my heart"? Are we able to say of someone else, "How I yearn . . . for you with the affection of Jesus Christ"? (Philippians 1:8).

FEBRUARY 14

Hear, O earth: behold, I will bring evil upon this people, even the fruit of their thoughts (JEREMIAH 6:19a).

"The fruit of their thoughts." This is a searching phrase. God, who sees into the heart, knew that Israel's defection from Him had begun in the inner life. And so His omniscient warning of judgment was simply that their thoughts would find real embodiment. Pause a moment, and ask yourself how you would like all your thoughts to bear fruit. It will not take you long to understand the probing nature of this warning. There is only one source of safety from the dangerous tyranny of thought. It is submission to the Holy Spirit who alone can bring into captivity every thought to the obedience of Christ.

FEBRUARY 15

Jesus had compassion on them, and touched their eyes: and immediately their eyes received sight, and they followed him (MATTHEW 20:34).

Every individual who is born again through faith in the Lord Jesus has passed from darkness into light: once blind and unable to discern spiritual things, the eyes of his heart have been enlightened. Why? For what purpose has God given us spiritual insight? Has He given it to us only that we may become more and more expert at the intricacies of Bible study? No. For while we do need His guidance in understanding the Word, our Lord also opens the eyes of our hearts, so that we may become more and more expert in following Him, in serving our fellowmen, and in doing His will in everything.

FEBRUARY 16

Nevertheless I have somewhat against thee, because thou hast left thy first love (REVELATION 2:4).

With two exceptions the risen Christ tells each of the seven churches of Asia (chapters 2 and 3) that He has something against it. In the case of this first message, what our Lord has against the church of Ephesus is its waning affection for Himself. "Thou hast left thy first love."

The Ephesian church was a flourishing one. According to tradition, the beloved disciple himself lived there in his later years and died there. But that church has long since gone. The ancient city of Ephesus is in ruins. Its candlestick has been removed. Why? Well, we do not have any record in Scripture that Ephesus was doctrinally corrupt. We only know that it grew cold in its love for Christ. So it stands as a warning against any cooling of Christian devotion. Not that our first love for the Saviour must keep on manifesting itself in the same way through the years. It may develop quietly, for the deepening of love may go on unobtrusively. But spiritual formalism and coldness of heart are different. Persisted in, they impose the silence of death upon a Christian testimony in our day just as when Ephesus was flourishing.

FEBRUARY 17

We will not hide them from their children, showing to the generation to come the praises of the Lord, and his strength, and his wonderful works that he hath done (PSALM 78:4).

Here is a word from God about education. The school that would hide from its pupils the fundamentals of secular knowledge would be inexcusably remiss. But what of education that hides from the children entrusted to its care "the praises of the Lord, and his strength, and his wonderful works"? The church of Christ has a teaching duty; it cannot hide the things of God from youth. And so vast is the spiritual illiteracy of American youth that it will take more than the weekly Sunday School period to dispel it. Christian education is one of the most productive forms of outreach. Are you supporting it by your gifts and prayers and by your personal participation in its work? And you parents, is Christian education really going on in your home?

FEBRUARY 18

For as many as are led by the Spirit of God, they are the sons of God (ROMANS 8:14).

You are a Christian. Ask yourself, then, this question: "Who led me to Christ?" "Why", you say, "such and such a person led me to Christ"; and you mention a pastor, a relative, or friend, thinking of the person who brought you the Gospel at the time you were saved.

This is the human answer. God does use His servants in leading people to Christ, but it is not God's servants who do the leading. There is another who leads us to Christ. He is the Holy Spirit. Every person who has been born again has been led by Him and Him alone to the Saviour.

Surely this is what Paul means when he says, "For as many as are led by the Spirit of God, they are the sons of God." No man is able in himself to convert another man or work the miracle of regeneration. Only God the Holy Spirit does these things. So let us recognize this first of all by giving thanks to Him who has regenerated us. And let us also recognize it in our testimony, so that we may never trust in our own perseverance, or logic, or zeal in witnessing for Christ.

FEBRUARY 19

He hath said, I will never leave thee, nor forsake thee (HE-BREWS 13:5b).

What word shall we emphasize here? What word indeed, unless the first one, "He"? The whole meaning of this beautiful sentence depends upon who said it. It would be small help simply to have just any human being tell us, "I will never leave you nor forsake you." Oh yes, if we were completely alone, the companionship of almost anyone would mean something. But how much more it means when somebody we love promises never to leave us. Love makes such a statement very precious. But think, Christian, of the wonderful fact that none other than the Lord Himself is saying to you, "I will never leave thee nor forsake thee." The closest human tie is only for life. The Lord's promise is for this life and for eternity. He has really said it. He means what He has said. He will never leave you, nor forsake you.

FEBRUARY 20

Rejoice in the Lord, ye righteous; and give thanks at the remembrance of his holiness (PSALM 97:12).

No man can enter fully into the worship of God, unless he recognizes that true worship is a joyous thing. As the psalmist said elsewhere, "I was glad when they said unto me, Let us go into the house of the Lord" (Psalm 122:1). Every minister, particularly the preacher who has frequently addressed congregations other than his own, will confirm the fact that many people come to church with staid and solemn expressions on their faces. Now and then, however, as one looks out over a congregation, he sees countenances that fairly radiate Christian joy. Just to glance at such worshipers is an inspiration to better preaching. Reverence is essential to worship. Yet nowhere does the Bible say that reverence and joy are incompatible. Truly the worship and giving of thanks to God, whether done publicly or privately, should be one of our most joyful experiences.

FEBRUARY 21

And at the same time there arose no small stir about that way (ACTS 19:23). that Jesus taught

One of the distressing things about many of us Christians is that we create so little stir. We are so placid and sleepy that the world pays little attention to us. Sin flourishes unrebuked around us; in our communities lives are being blighted and souls lost, and we do not seem to be greatly concerned. The Gospel, the "dynamic" of God (Romans 1:16), is exciting. The "way" is "a new and living way" (Hebrews 10:19, 20). And when it challenges sin, it cannot help but create a stir. Mere "sound and fury" have no place in the Christian life, and neither has apathy. If we believers would only wake up and live for Christ, what a holy stir we would make!

FEBRUARY 22

For what nation is there so great, who hath God so nigh unto them, as the Lord our God is in all things that we call upon him for? (DEUTERONOMY 4:7).

Here is the true measure of greatness. That measure is not material achievement but nearness to God. In the scale of eternal values Israel was a very great nation. Though small in size she was great in her covenant-relation to God. This was due to God's grace, not Israel's own virtue.

In His grace, God has given our land a great spiritual and moral heritage. We who are Christians need to learn from the history of Israel the danger of apostasy. Should we not be witnessing to the primary importance of the individual's relationship to God? Should we not be concerned about justice and righteousness among our people. No nation can be truly great in the Lord's sight whose people are far off from the God of all love and wisdom and grace. No nation can endure that persists in going its own way apart from reliance upon the living God.

FEBRUARY 23

And the two disciples heard him speak, and they followed Jesus (JOHN 1:37).

So it is that disciples are made. In most cases it is through hearing some spoken witness to the Lord Jesus. What, then, did John the Baptist say of Him? Well, if we read the preceding verse, we see that John's witness was very simple: "He looked at Jesus as he walked and said, 'Behold the Lamb of God'" (v. 36, RSV). Just five words, yet they were enough. Does your witness contain them? It's all very well to speak of Christ as a great teacher, an outstanding ethical leader, the finest flower of the human race. But that is not sufficient. No witness for Him is complete unless it presents Him as "the Lamb of God"—that is, as the Saviour who died for the sin of the world. There is no Christianity without sacrifice; there can be no real witness without the cross.

FEBRUARY 24

And Shema begot Raham, the father of Jorkoam: and Rekem begot Shammai (1 CHRONICLES 2:44).

Who today knows anything of these and the many others whose names are written down in this section of Scripture? But what joys and sorrows are wrapped up in each name! They were men and women as we are. They had their temptations and victories, their failures and successes. They suffered, as do you and I. And then they died, as we shall unless the Lord comes in our lifetime. Through it all they were known to God. In His providence He called the chronicler to write down their names, the obscure alongside the eminent.

It is one of the lessons of the genealogies that the eminent come from the obscure. No matter how great a man may become, he must rise from the common level of mankind. Moreover, we see in this procession of unknown Hebrews the very stuff of which history is made. History is not a mere succession of events; it is the sum total of the lives and actions of myriads of human beings, as God's purpose is worked out in and through them The Bible is a personal Book, concerned with individual men and women. God is a personal God, and He cares about people like you and me.

FEBRUARY 25

The silver is mine, and the gold is mine, saith the Lord of hosts (HAGGAI 2:8).

If this is true, and assuredly it is, failure to give generously to God's work is a serious thing. For poor stewardship amounts to nothing less than withholding from the Lord that which is His. Have you ever taken your salary or income, placed it before God and said to Him, "This is yours, O Lord. Show me how to use it"? Do you know what it is to take the Lord into your finances, personal as well as business or professional? Is Christ the Lord of your bank account and of your pocketbook?

FEBRUARY 26

Or if a soul touch any unclean thing . . . he also shall be unclean, and guilty (LEVITICUS 5:2).

To the modern mind, steeped in secularism and with little understanding of the biblical conception of sin, such legal provisions as are set forth not only here but in many other places in the Pentateuch are almost unintelligible. But to the believer, whose conscience is tender respecting sin, there is much he can understand. For one thing, there is the great lesson that sin is important, so important that something must be done about it The whole long ritual of animal sacrifices and offerings points to Christ who Himself became "a full, perfect, and sufficient sacrifice, oblation, and satisfaction, for the sins of the whole world" (Book of Common Prayer).

There are many subsidiary teachings of this ritual. Consider, for example, the contagious power of evil. Ancient Israel took defilement, even in an outward, physical aspect, very seriously. Their ceremonial uncleanness was representative of spiritual defilement. And they were right. One transgression begets another. An impure thought or evil word has a way of reproducing itself. One of the sure marks of the divine character of the worship of ancient Israel is that it recognized the sinfulness of sin.When we acknowledge that sin is always a serious matter, we have taken a great step forward in godly living.

FEBRUARY 27

You who fear the Lord, trust in the Lord! (PSALM 115:11, RSV).

One may fear God and yet be unregenerate. Without doubt there are non-Christians who, reverencing the Almighty, stand in deep awe of His greatness. They have taken the first step toward coming to Him. But the first step is not enough. If the fear of the Lord is the beginning of wisdom, then trust in the Lord makes us wise in appropriating His gift of salvation. No one who fails to fear God will really trust Him. Similarly, no one who fully trusts Him can fail to fear Him. Because God is great and holy, because God is powerful and infinitely just, because God is all-wise and all-seeing, He should have our complete trust. The fear of the Lord is the foundation of worship; trust in the Lord is worship resulting in a personal hold upon the Holy One. Without trust worship is dead; without reverence, trust is presumptuous.

FEBRUARY 28

No man is sure of life (JOB 24:22b).

This little remark, which is part of Job's answer to Eliphaz, contains a very big meaning. "No man is sure of life." Physically the truth of that assertion is undeniable. As James puts it, "What is your life? It is even a vapour, that appeareth for a little time, and then vanisheth away" (James 4:14). No matter how strong our health, the uncertainty of human existence is so great that none of us is assured of holding on to this present life.

"No man is sure of life." But there is another realm in which that statement is not true. It does not apply to the Christian and eternal life. What Job in his perplexity could not see, because he was on the other side of the cross, we believers know. Because of the redemption purchased by the blood of our Saviour and validated by His resurrection, we may be sure of eternal life. Granted that the duration of our earthly existence is uncertain, how wonderful it is to know that there is nothing uncertain about eternal life. By faith in Christ we have eternal life, not only today but forever. It is the blessed prerogative of every Christian to say, humbly and gratefully, "Through God's grace I am sure of life for evermore."

FEBRUARY 29

*But I will warn you whom to fear: fear him who, after he
has killed, has power to cast into hell; yes, I tell you,
fear him! Are not five sparrows sold for two pennies? And
not one of them is forgotten before God. Why, even the
hairs of your head are all numbered. Fear not; you are of
more value than many sparrows* (LUKE 12:5, 6, 7, RSV).

"Fear him. . . . Fear not." Why these two apparently contradictory exhortations so close together? Well, fear may be wholesome provided we are afraid of the right person or thing. Our
Lord is telling us that no Christian need fear men, for the most
men can do is kill the body (v. 4). But there is another who,
"after he has killed, has power to cast into hell." "Yes," Christ
continues, "I tell you, fear him." And who is this being of such
power? "Satan, of course," some reply. But that answer will not
do. For there is only One who has power to cast into hell, and
He is the God who will one day consign Satan himself to the
lake of fire. The Lord Jesus is therefore giving us the twofold
lesson of courage toward men but fear toward God. We need
that lesson, because all of us are prone to fear men and be brave
toward God.

Furthermore our Lord goes on to give us not the opposite but
the complementary truth, beautifully introducing it by His
personal assurance that God remembers the sparrows and numbers the very hairs of our heads. So He is teaching us that, despite the opposition of men and even of Satan, more powerful
than any adversary is God who is great enough to protect even
the least of us.

MARCH 1

And being fully persuaded that, what he had promised, he was able also to perform (ROMANS 4:21).

Here we see the secret of Abraham's greatness. It is simply that he was a man who took God at His word. Because Abraham was fully persuaded that what God has promised He is able to do, he is the outstanding example of faith in all history. God signally honored that faith and gave Abraham the promise that in him all nations of the earth would be blessed.

Suppose that some friend or relative promises us a certain thing. If we refuse to accept this promise, the implication may be that the one who makes it is untrustworthy. So with us and God. To deny the promises of the Almighty insults His divine integrity. No one can occupy higher spiritual ground than that of simply being a believer. No mysticism or pietism is so acceptable to God as Abraham's attitude of being fully persuaded of God's ability to do everything He has promised.

MARCH 2

The scripture of truth (DANIEL 10:21a).

This phrase has a unique source, coming as it does from the supernatural being who appeared to Daniel in his vision. "The scripture of truth." Only one Book can meet that designation. There are many scriptures, for the word simply means "writing." There are even other "sacred" scriptures. But only to one can the word "truth" be applied from beginning to end. In respect to truth, all other writings are relative, but God's Word is absolute. Despite nearly two thousand years of attacks upon it, Christ's own characterization of Scripture has never been superseded: "Thy word is truth (John 17:17).

Are you utilizing Scripture daily through believing it, depending on it, obeying it, and living it?

MARCH 3

Faith which worketh by love (GALATIANS 5:6a).

It was James Clerk Maxwell, the great English physicist, who said that there never was a theory of the universe that did not need a god to make it go. And it is equally true that there is no system of Christian belief that does not need love to make it effective. Not reverence, nor fear, nor even hope of reward is the chief motive for Christians to translate their faith into action. These all have their place, but greater than any of them is the true motive of spiritual service—the love of Christ that constrains us to bear witness to Him and to do His work in the world.

MARCH 4

The Lord bless thee, and keep thee: The Lord make his face shine upon thee, and be gracious unto thee: The Lord lift up his countenance upon thee, and give thee peace (NUMBERS 6:24-26).

This is the first of the great scripture benedictions. It has never been superseded or surpassed, though there are New Testament benedictions worthy to stand beside it in beauty.

Christians may see between the lines of this benediction the truth of the Trinity. Three times the Lord's name is mentioned. Not only that, but the three blessings associated with this triple mention are each of them befitting the three persons of the Trinity. It is God the Father to whom we look for blessing and security. It is God the Son who illuminates our lives, whose face we shall one day see in all its glory (1 John 3:2), and who is our King of grace. It is God the Holy Spirit who fulfills the blessing for us by putting in our hearts the peace that passes understanding. Surely the words of this benediction are among the greatest spiritual treasures the Bible contains. If you don't know them by heart, learn them today.

MARCH 5

Come with us, and we will do you good (NUMBERS 10:29, RSV).

It is Moses speaking, and he is talking to his brother-in-law, Hobab. First he says to him, "We are setting out for the place of which the Lord said, I will give it to you." Then he invites Hobab to accompany them, promising to do him good. Finally he states the reason for this promise by saying, "The Lord has promised good to Israel."

Such an invitation may be given by every Christian to his non-Christian friends. All who are in Christ are "setting out for the place of which the Lord said, I will give it to you." Israel was on the way to the promised land; we are on the way to our heavenly home. And if we invite others to join us, surely we also may promise, as Moses promised Hobab, to do them good. We may promise this because our Lord has many times spoken good of us, who are part of His Church. As the hymn says, "Glorious things of thee are spoken, Zion, City of our God."

MARCH 6

And Solomon brought up the daughter of Pharaoh out of the city of David unto the house that he had built for her: for he said, My wife shall not dwell in the house of David king of Israel, because the places are holy, whereunto the ark of the Lord hath come (2 CHRONICLES 8:11).

Solomon had taken the daughter of Pharaoh in marriage. Yet he could not bring himself to introduce her into David's palace in Jerusalem, which had been sanctified by the presence of the ark of the Lord. So he did what some Christians today are vainly trying to do. He tried to compartmentalize his life. But it did not work. This king who began so nobly and brilliantly ended up ignobly and in darkness. Let every one of us Christians remember that it is impossible for us to keep segregated in our lives anything that displeases God. Such things simply won't stay where we want them to. They will grow, their influence will ramify, till one day we shall wake up to find our lives ruined. True holiness means wholeness in living for the Lord Jesus. It demands separation from anyone or anything we cannot introduce to the Holy Spirit who dwells within us

MARCH 7

And he saith unto them, Follow me, and I will make you fishers of men (MATTHEW 4:19).

When our Lord called out to Peter and Andrew, "Follow me," He was speaking to us all. And this is what He is saying: "Follow me and I will make you . . ." Yes, we follow Christ. We leave personal ambitions. We turn our backs on our own interests and follow our Lord. Then He shows Himself the great moulder of lives. He takes control and begins to work. He takes us as we are and makes us his own men and women.

Let us not fear his controlling touch. To follow Christ and have Him form our lives for His service means not narrower but expanded opportunities. The Lord's plans are as various as people themselves. He is able to use everyone of us to His glory.

MARCH 8   1922337

He knew what was in man (JOHN 2:25b).

Early in his account of our Lord's public ministry, John states this great truth. The Lord Jesus *knew* man. No one—philosopher, scientist, physician, or saint—has ever had anything approaching His understanding of the human heart. A thoughtful reading of the Gospel records shows a depth of insight into human character and motives unapproached by any other leader, past or present.

But why talk about this only in the past tense? Every Christian knows that Jesus Christ is the living Lord and Saviour. He who long years ago knew what was in the heart of man knows men today just as intimately as when He walked and talked in Palestine. How often we long for understanding! There are times when loneliness comes over us, as we realize that not even our best beloved understand us fully. Then is when companionship with the Lord Jesus is so helpful. Fellowship with Him means walking daily with a divine Friend who has complete knowledge of all things and with whom we may share everything, no matter how hidden from other persons. "He knew what was in man." Praise God for such a Saviour!

MARCH 9

And Jacob served seven years for Rachel; and they seemed unto him but a few days, for the love he had to her (GENESIS 29:20).

The story of Jacob's sojourn with his uncle Laban shows him experiencing treatment like that he had given his brother Esau. No sooner had he begun to live with Laban than he became the victim of the wily Syrian's avarice. God was teaching Jacob that self-will does not pay. But along with the shadows of discipline there was the sunshine of love. The seven years Jacob served for Rachel passed quickly "for the love he had to her."

So should it be with Christian life and service. Many a missionary finds his term of seven years passing swiftly "for the love" he has for Christ. Many a veteran preacher looks back over a lifetime spent in the ministry of the King of kings and it seems to him "but a few days," because he has been serving for the love of Christ. Many a faithful Sunday school teacher or church officer recalls years of service and thinks how quickly they have passed. Christian service may be hard; sometimes it brings great testing. But it is not tiresome when done for the love we have for our Lord Jesus.

MARCH 10

Rend your heart, and not your garments, and turn unto the Lord your God (JOEL 2:13a).

This is simply another way of saying that God wants a change of heart, not just a change of externals. However much man may be impressed with outward religious demonstration, God looks on the heart. The rending of the clothes, the overt emotionalism of a certain kind of religious activity, or the elaborate ritual of another kind—all these are futile if the heart is not touched. God is honored only by broken and contrite hearts, not by strained voices or torn garments.

We have liberty in our forms of worship, and rightly so. But whatever kind of worship we follow, let us be sure that it comes from our hearts and honors God and His Son.

MARCH 11

They gave after their ability (EZRA 2:69a).

It was a great task Zerubbabel and the thousands with him faced. But first of all they needed practical support for rebuilding the Lord's temple. We do not know the names of "chief of the fathers" (v. 68) who came forward with their gifts. But we cannot help being impressed by the quality of stewardship they showed. Ezra says that they "offered freely for the house of God" and that "they gave after their ability." No one can do more than that. We need a like spirit in relation to the support of the Lord's work. Have you ever sat down and honestly considered whether you are really giving in accord with your ability?

MARCH 12

And I beheld, and, lo, in the midst of the throne and of the four beasts, and in the midst of the elders, stood a Lamb as it had been slain, having seven horns and seven eyes, which are the seven Spirits of God sent forth into all the earth (REVELATION 5:6).

In this chapter John is enabled to look closely at the throne in heaven. Doing so, he sees who is in its midst. It is "a Lamb as it had been slain." That Lamb is our Saviour in glory. And the words, "as it had been slain," symbolize the fact that He took back to heaven with Him in His glorified body the marks of our redemption. When we see Him in heaven, we shall recognize Him by the nail prints in His hands and feet, and by His wounded side.

In a very particular way, Revelation is the book of the Lamb. A glance at a concordance proves this. The word "lamb" in reference to Christ occurs twice in the Gospel of John, once each in Acts and 1 Peter, and nowhere else in the New Testament apart from Revelation. But in Revelation it is found twenty-seven times. Truly this last book of the Bible is uniquely that of the Lamb. The Holy Spirit, who inspired the Scriptures, makes no mistakes in emphasis. Therefore we may be sure that His placing this final emphasis upon the Lamb means that our Lord's sacrificial work is of central and of eternal significance. Is the Lamb of God central in your worship?

MARCH 13

They that are Christ's have crucified the flesh with the affections and lusts (GALATIANS 5:24).

There is a searching implication in the very form of this sentence. It is a clear, declarative statement. Paul sets down as a fact of Christian experience that the flesh is crucified. In other words, he takes it for granted that the passions and lusts of us Christians are nailed to the cross. Yes, we say, that is true theologically. Our old nature was crucified with Him. But is it true in our experience? How revealing it is that these teachings about death to sin and the crucifixion of self should be known as "the deeper truths," when they are in reality facts of normal Christian experience available in power to every believer!

MARCH 14

But we all, with [unveiled] face beholding as in a glass the glory of the Lord, are changed into the same image from glory to glory (2 CORINTHIANS 3:18).

Looking is a very simple thing. It does not require great ability or education. It just needs the desire to turn your eyes to a certain person or thing, and, in the case of beholding, to keep them there. Any Christian may behold his Lord, providing he takes the time to do so.

But the kind of beholding Paul speaks of requires the "unveiled face." What is it, then, that veils the face from Christ? Well, unbelief certainly draws a curtain between His glory and our hearts. Similarly, unconfessed sin is bound to obscure His face.

At the heart of Christian character is the lifelong beholding of Christ. Oh, that we might take time to be alone with our Lord and His Word, to bow before Him in prayerful adoration, to unveil our faces before "the Sun of righteousness" (Malachi 4:2)! Our appointments for today may be many. But there is one indispensable appointment for which we must allow, and that is the quiet time when, with the unveiled face of faith, we look to the Lord Jesus.

MARCH 15

Say, I am your sign (Ezekiel 12:11a).

God addressed these words to Ezekiel. He had just told
him to move his belongings before all the people as a symbolic
action of their going into captivity. Then, when they asked him,
"What doest thou?" (v. 9) he was to reply, "I am your sign."

We Christians are Ezekiels to the world about us. We are
signs of the Lord and the faith we profess. With us it is not a
matter of dramatic symbol but of consistent living. Every minister is a sign to his congregation, every father and mother to their
children, every business or professional person to those they
come in contact with. Are you a sign of Christ for your neighbors?

MARCH 16

*And unto man he said, Behold, the fear of the Lord, that
is wisdom; and to depart from evil is understanding* (Job
28:28).

From the literary point of view, there are few more beautiful
places in the Old Testament than this twenty-eighth chapter
of Job. The flow of the words and the vividness of the figures
delight both ear and mind. What brings the chapter to its climax is the section where Job, having described the hidden
treasures of the earth, turns to something more precious than
gold. Wisdom, he declares, lies in the fear of the Lord, and in
goodness there is lasting enlightenment. Solomon put this same
truth in his Proverbs; it is found in the Psalms and has since
been repeated countless times.

Yet men have not learned the lesson; today as never before
they seem determined to seek wisdom apart from God. Human
reason cannot by itself solve world problems. No science, philosophy, or theories of government can supersede the understanding that God has linked with goodness and integrity. Unless men are willing through God's help to depart from evil,
their thinking is bound to be warped and their understanding
darkened. Job spoke the unchanging truth. "The fear of the
Lord, that is wisdom; and to depart from evil is understanding."

MARCH 17

"Salvation is of the Jews (JOHN 4:22b).

Here is the final answer to anti-Semitism. Let the ignorant and bigoted, the misguided and malevolent, hate the Jew. Nevertheless, the fact remains that, as our Lord said, "Salvation is of the Jews." Nothing can alter this. Out of Israel came Christ. And Christ is the Saviour of the world. He only, He and no other, is "the way, the truth, and the life." Through Him alone men come to the Father.

There is much in anti-Semitism that makes it almost the ultimate in wickedness. To hate and persecute those whom God used to bring salvation to the lost world is a crime. Yet it is a crime even Christians may fall into. Its best preventive is an enlightened knowledge of the Scriptures. A Christian who knows the Word of God and is taught by the Holy Spirit ought never fall into this sin of despising the people from whom our Lord came. Let us remember that the human ancestry of our blessed Saviour has deep Old Testament roots. Let us love and pray for our Jewish brothers, let us minister to their suffering and need when they are oppressed, and let us share with them what Christ means to us.

MARCH 18

Ye are . . . the epistle of Christ . . . written not with ink, but with the Spirit of the living God; not in tables of stone, but in fleshly tables of the heart (2 CORINTHIANS 3:2, 3).

Thus Paul answers those who are attacking the validity of his ministry. "I need," he was saying, "no letters of recommendation. The Corinthian Christians are my living letters of recommendation." What an essential truth he brings out! Most Christians do not write books, but day by day they are publishing lives. The world that scorns to read the Bible will read them and in reading them—if the living epistles are true to their Lord—will learn something of Christ. Publishing a printed book is a matter of choice; publishing a life, yes, your own life of Christ, is inescapable. Oh, for a higher quality of living, walking Christian literature!

MARCH 19

*And they that know thy name will put their trust in thee,
for thou, Lord, hast not forsaken them that seek thee*
(PSALM 9:10).

The Psalter in the Book of Common Prayer has this beautiful translation of the last clause of this verse: "For thou, Lord, hast never failed them that seek thee." Man fails those who look to man. Fix your eyes, pin your hopes entirely on any human being, no matter how fine and exalted that person may be, and you are liable to some form of disillusion. But fix your eyes on Jesus, seek Him with your whole heart, and you will find that David spoke truly when he wrote these words. God does not fail them that seek Him. The trouble is that we so seldom really seek Him. Is it your deepest desire to know Him in every portion of your life? Then you may count on Him never to fail you.

MARCH 20

*Accept one another, then, just as Christ accepted you,
in order to bring praise to God* (ROMANS 15:7, NIV).

The context of this verse refers to the spiritual unity of Jewish and Gentile Christians. In principle, however, it applies to all believers everywhere. Whatever the differences may be, Paul is teaching, there must not be any barriers to fellowship between those who are in the body of Christ. For our Lord has received our fellow Christians to the glory of God, and if He has received them, how can we who have also been received by Him refuse to have anything to do with any among them? Before the transcendent fact of Christ's acceptance, barriers must fall. The gap between Jew and Gentile is a real one, but in Christ it is bridged. So today no difference of race, social position, or anything else can be allowed to hinder the mutual acceptance of those who are truly accepted in Christ "where is neither Greek nor Jew, circumcision nor uncircumcision, Barbarian, Scythian, bond nor free; but Christ is all, and in all" (Colossians 3:11).

MARCH 21

Having been kept by the Holy Spirit from preaching the word in the province of Asia . . . they tried to enter Bithynia; but the Spirit of Jesus would not allow them to (Acts 16:6, 7, NIV).

Paul and his companions must have been sincerely perplexed. Their desire was a good one; they wished to preach the Word in certain places. But the Spirit Himself checked them. Why? Because He had a greater goal to reach. And so, because Paul was obedient to the guidance of the Holy Spirit at this point in his ministry, the Gospel went over into Europe.

Are you blocked in performing what seems to you a good work for God? Does your witness appear to be held back and your service seem to be comparatively fruitless? Don't be distressed, provided that you are really in the place of obedience and readiness to do God's will in everything. Remember that your being blocked and held back may be the prelude of God's doing some greater work through you.

MARCH 22

And remember! I will be with you always, to the end of the world (Matthew 28:20, TEV).

Let us who belong to Christ claim this promise anew today. We have a right to do this, because our Lord spoke it as a personal promise. "I" and "you"—these are the two whom it concerns. It is the pledged word of the Lord of our life that He will never leave us or forsake us. He speaks it just as directly to us as He spoke it to His disciples long ago. To us He promises His presence all the days, not some of the days of our earthly pilgrimage.

Our bright days do not test this promise to the full; during them it is comparatively easy to believe that our Lord is with us. But the dark days, the days of disappointment and sorrow, of heartache and distress—they are the times when we need assurance. And the promise also holds for them. Christ's presence is a continuing presence; He will never leave those who trust in Him!

MARCH 23

The love awakened in you by the Spirit (COLOSSIANS 1:8, Williams).

Find a man who lives according to the biblical law of love and you have a man who is filled with the Spirit. For love proceeds from the Spirit of Christ. One of the most searching tests of our discipleship is whether or not it is rooted and grounded in love. Let us not forget that the Word of God drastically repudiates the loveless disciple. "Now if any man have not the Spirit of Christ, he is none of his," writes Paul (Romans 8:9b). Yes, the Spirit of Christ is the Spirit of love.

MARCH 24

If any of you lacks wisdom, he should ask God, who gives generously to all without finding fault, and it will be given to him (JAMES 1:5, NIV).

Our New Testament contains no more practical promise than this. Like so many Scripture promises, it is conditional. James says, "If any of you lacks wisdom." Yes, that relates to us all, for there is no one, no matter how learned or eminent, who does not lack wisdom. Even the wisest are as children when it comes to eternal things. More than that, our everyday lives are hedged about with ignorance. Not knowing the future, we cannot plan for it with absolute certainty. Not knowing the hearts of our fellow men, we need wisdom in dealing with them. We all qualify for this promise.

Now what does James say of the man who lacks wisdom? He says a very plain and at the same time profound thing. "He should ask God." How simple it is! You and I lack wisdom. We go to God and ask Him for it. God is the God "who," James reminds us, "gives generously to all without finding fault." Therefore, as we ask Him, He gives the wisdom we need.

Will you make this test the next time you need wisdom? Take James 1:5 and on the basis of this promise, ask God believingly (v. 6) for the wisdom you need. Then trust Him to answer you.

MARCH 25

Unto you therefore who believe he is precious (1 PETER 2:7).

How much do we value Christ? Is He really precious to us? He will be precious, provided that we do one thing—believe in Him.

There are many who know all about Christ and yet lack a Christian valuation of Him. Some admire Him, but He is not precious to them, for admiration is not enough. Others venerate Him, yet veneration does not lead to the valuation the apostle calls "precious." Many study Christ, but even intense study does not itself lead the heart to set that unique estimate upon Christ that looks on Him as precious. Where all these fail, belief succeeds. Belief succeeds, because true faith commits itself wholly to the Saviour. It has a vision of what it means to be lost without Christ. Knowing the meaning of salvation, it cannot but call Him who purchased our salvation with His own life's blood "precious."

MARCH 26

The fool says in his heart, "There is no God!" Their deeds are corrupt and vile, there is not one good man left. (PSALM 14:1, JB).

The message of this psalm, devoted so largely to the atheist, should not be passed over as obvious. If for no other reason than that our age is one of growing irreligion and contempt for God, we need to consider its message. Even in the opening verse there is a big lesson. First, the fool is characterized; he is portrayed not by what he does but by what he says in his heart. Not the outward word but the inner bent of the soul is in view. The atheist is a fool because he has made up his mind that there is no God. Then there follows a telling statement about those whose initial presupposition is the denial of God. Of such the psalmist says, "Their deeds are corrupt and vile, there is not one good man left." Consider the moral logic of this: first, an unbelieving heart brazenly declaring, "There is no God!"—then a corrupt life, wicked deeds, nothing good accomplished. Unpleasant to contemplate, these are the consequences of atheism

MARCH 27

He that spared not his own Son, but delivered him up for us all, how shall he not with him also freely give us all things? (ROMANS 8:32).

Nowhere is Paul's logic more impressively manifest than in Romans. He knew how to think with intensity and precision. Consider the logic of this great question. The reasoning is from the greater to the lesser Paul is arguing that God did not hesitate to give His own Son, but delivered Him up for us. How, then, shall we doubt that the God who went to that extent will not give us along with Christ all other things we need?

Remember that, O Christian, when you are in need. Think back to what God did in giving the Lord Jesus for you. Take courage in the fact that the God who went to such an infinite extent in your behalf can be trusted to do for you everything else that is necessary. The wonderful gift of the Lord Jesus Christ is God's guarantee that He will not let His own suffer the lack of any essential thing.

MARCH 28

And when the Lord saw that he turned aside to see, God called unto him out of the midst of the bush, and said, Moses, Moses. And he said, Here am I (EXODUS 3:4).

The scene is a desert in the vicinity of Mount Horeb. Moses has just looked at the burning bush. Now the Lord calls Moses by name and Moses answers in simple and full submission, "Here am I." In this incident we are brought face to face with one of the key places in world history. God was about to do great things to further His redemptive purpose in history. He might have summoned all the angels and archangels of heaven to carry out His purpose. But He willed it otherwise. He picked a fugitive shepherd, a man with a slow tongue, to lead His people out of bondage. Let us never doubt God's ability to use us to fulfill His purpose of blessing others through our lives, so long as, like Moses, we answer to His call with our own "Here am I."

MARCH 29

*His servants shall serve him. . . . they shall reign for ever
and ever* (REVELATION 22:3a, 5b).

These two statements speak volumes about the real nature of
heaven. First of all, they show us that it will be a place of
eternal service. While there is certainly rest in heaven, it will
hardly be the rest of inactivity. There will be tasks assigned,
things for the saints to do, and all will be in the service of the
King. So we may affirm that there will be nothing of boredom
in the eternal home of the redeemed. In this better land happiness will be unending, and surely much of it will spring
from the joy of serving the King of kings and Lord of lords.

Then again we see that heaven is a place of everlasting victory. "They shall reign forever and ever." Service is linked to
victory! This life is a time of conflict from beginning to end.
But in heaven the conflict will be resolved. Through Him who
has put all things under His feet we too shall reign.

MARCH 30

*And all this assembly shall know that the Lord saveth not
with sword and spear; for the battle is the Lord's, and he
will give you into our hands* (1 SAMUEL 17:47).

These words conclude David's answer to Goliath's challenge.
David is confident of victory, not because he is trusting in a
sword or shield, but because of the power of the Name of the
Lord of Hosts (v. 45). He knows that Goliath will be over-
thrown and with his defeat the Philistines routed. He knows
this, not because he himself is strong, but because God is on
his side. There is much that is fine in David's words, but nothing more inspiring than this declaration: "The battle is the
Lord's." David's struggle with Goliath may well illustrate our
daily encounter with the enemy of our souls. What a comfort
to realize that we need never engage in this battle single-
handed. David was right; "The battle is the Lord's." For every
believer it is true that the Lord of hosts is on his side.

"The battle is the Lord's." Believing this more fully will bring
us greater peace of heart leading to more effective service for
our King.

MARCH 31

*Then he said unto them, O fools, and slow of heart to be-
lieve all that the prophets have spoken* (LUKE 24:25).

It is a mistake to think that we may pick and choose how
much of God's revelation we care to believe. When God speaks,
He means to be completely believed by those He addresses.
Here we see two disciples on the road to Emmaus. Our risen
Lord joins them, but they do not know Him and continue to
voice their perplexity over His death and the reports of His
appearances after it. Then He Himself interrupts them with
this rebuke.

Notice that the rebuke centers around the word "all." These
two disciples were not unbelievers. They were sincerely concerned about Christ. But they were all at sea. And the reason
was that they did not believe enough about Christ; they were
"slow of heart to believe all that the prophets had spoken."

How is it with us? Are we these days perplexed and troubled?
Then let us ask ourselves whether we are believing "all that the
prophets have spoken" concerning God's Son. You see, we may
believe what is written regarding His birth, and life, and death,
and resurrection, and yet miss some things God would also have
us know. For the prophets assure us that there is a glorious future for the children of God. They tell us to look up and await
the coming of our Lord. May we be delivered from that slow-
ness of heart which refuses to believe "all that the prophets have
spoken" concerning our Lord Jesus Christ.

APRIL 1

Love never fails (1 CORINTHIANS 13:8, NIV).

How can love fail? It is the principle by which the Lord Jesus Christ Himself worked. It defines God. It is the motive that led to our redemption.

Just giving love the pre-eminence in human relationships—placing it above persuasion, threatening, or argument—following this method would result in overcoming many antagonisms and hatreds. Love can solve most of our problems with others and theirs with us. Oh, that our Lord's own love might be more fully shed abroad in our hearts!

APRIL 2

And I, if I be lifted up from the earth, will draw all men unto me (JOHN 12:32).

It may well be said that the New Testament contains no more reassuring word for the witnessing Christian than this. It is a declaration of spiritual law, and Christ Himself gives it to us. It sets forth an inevitable sequence of cause and effect. The cause is the lifting up of the Lord Jesus, which took place on Calvary. The effect is the drawing of mankind to Him who was thus lifted up. And today, nearly 2,000 years later, our task as witnesses follows this sequence. We are to proclaim Christ crucified. We are to proclaim Him as the risen and living Saviour. That is our task. The rest will be done by our Lord. For ultimately it is He Himself, the Lord of life, who draws men. The message is essential, but it is not the Saviour. Only the Lord has power over the souls of men. To be sure, not every one we witness to will come to Him, for there are some who will not listen. But there are those who will come, because they are drawn by the living Lord. Let us not be discouraged. If we are faithful in proclaiming Christ crucified, He will draw men to Himself.

APRIL 3

For he is thy Lord; and worship thou him (PSALM 45:11b).

Church services often begin with a "Call to Worship." Here is such a call. This simple statement is like a hand pointing toward heaven. It directs our hearts to Christ, the King, who has already been described in this Psalm in all His perfection. It says in effect, "Look at Him; He, and no other, is your Lord." And as we look at Him, we see that the remainder of the sentence is inevitable. Nothing prepares the heart more for worship of the Lord than to contemplate His beauty and perfection. When we see Him and realize that He is our Lord, then we are ready to adore Him. A good look at the Lord Jesus fits the soul for worship.

APRIL 4

Woe to them that are at ease in Zion, and trust in the mountain of Samaria, which are named chief of the nations, to whom the house of Israel came! (AMOS 6:1).

"Woe to them that are at ease in Zion." What does Amos mean? Without doubt he is warning those who, in a time of shameful perversion of justice and callous exploitation of the underprivileged, were contented in their luxury and indolence. After all, there are times when ease is wrong and when godly people cannot sit idly by and see the weak oppressed. Callous unconcern when crimes are being committed and injustice perpetrated is abhorrent to God. And it is peculiarly a sin of the comfortably religious. How easy it is to sit "at ease in Zion" without lifting up either hand or voice against the abuses of the day! We Christians who are committed to taking the Bible seriously ought to recover something of Amos's burning indignation against evil, remembering Peter's word that "judgment must begin at the house of God" (1 Peter 4:17).

APRIL 5

As thy days, so shall thy strength be (DEUTERONOMY 33:25b).

The Bible contains few more encouraging words than these. Moses had been blessing the tribes of Israel. Then he continued with this wonderful promise: "As thy days, so shall thy strength be." What more can anyone ask? God knows our days and measures them with divine precision. But He does more; He promises that our strength will be proportionate to our need. It is not only a promise of duration but one of quality; when our days become hard and trying, then our strength will be of the kind needed for that special testing.

We cannot predict either the nature or number of our days. But unpredictable as the future is, we may go forward with confidence, knowing that God who remains faithful has promised strength according to our daily needs.

APRIL 6

In that night did God appear unto Solomon, and said unto him, Ask what I shall give thee (2 CHRONICLES 1:7).

Have you ever thought that the Lord Jesus gives us a similar invitation? He said to His disciples and through them to us, "Ask and it shall be given you; seek, and ye shall find; knock, and it shall be opened unto you" (Luke 11:9). And He also said, "Whatever you ask in my name, I will do it, that the Father may be glorified in the Son; if you ask anything in my name, I will do it" (John 14:13, 14, RSV).

The significant thing with us, just as with Solomon, is *what* we are asking for. Are we asking God for spiritual gifts—for wisdom, love, patience, and all the other manifestations of the spiritual life that should grace the true Christian? Or is most of our prayer time made up of seeking to get things from God. Not that it is wrong to pray for the smallest of our physical and material needs. But what has the first place in our prayers? Christ's beatitude that assures us that those who hunger and thirst after righteousness shall be blessed has never been annulled. It is a great privilege to have access to God in prayer. But oh, that we might make better use of it!

APRIL 7

I have stuck unto thy testimonies (PSALM 119:31a).

Evidently the author of these words was in trouble, for he immediately added "O Lord, put me not to shame" (v. 31b). His ground for pleading in difficulty was simply that he had really adhered to God's Word. Have you done that? Could you tell God right now that you have stuck to His Book? You see, it is not a matter of a sudden action but rather the habit of months and years. The time element is involved. Happy are those who, through daily reading of Scripture and through practising what they read, stick daily to their Lord's commands.

APRIL 8

Verily I say unto you, Except ye be converted, and become as little children, ye shall not enter into the kingdom of heaven (MATTHEW 18:3).

The world has changed vastly since Christ said that. But the condition for entrance into the kingdom of heaven remains exactly the same. No increase of scientific and technical knowledge or any new theological insights can alter the requirement that only through conversion and the willingness to become as little children can we enter the kingdom of heaven.

There are those who say that individual redemption must be supplanted by service in society. But Christ's words have not changed. Service is essential; but it comes after, not before conversion. Jesus says to all of us, "Except ye be converted, and become as little children, ye shall not enter into the kingdom of heaven." Some may speak of building the kingdom regardless of one's personal relationship to Christ. The fact remains that you must be in the kingdom if you are to work for it. And we enter it only on Christ's terms

APRIL 9

And I, brethren, when I came to you, came not with excellency of speech or of wisdom, declaring unto you the testimony of God. For I determined not to know anything among you, save Jesus Christ, and him crucified (1 CORINTHIANS 2:1, 2).

Corinth was one of the most difficult places Paul was called to preach in. There, if anywhere, he might have had an excuse for compromise. But there he spoke with unusual definiteness. So he made it plain at the beginning of this letter that he had but one central theme. In favor of this theme, Paul was willing to give up all temptation to eloquence and put aside all display of learning. He would proclaim Jesus Christ and Him crucified, and he would do it with singleness of heart.

This is great spiritual strategy. Would that we today might follow it more closely. A difficult assignment for witness, an audience not naturally sympathetic to the Gospel, a group of people so learned that we fear that the truth of Christ will not attract them—what are these but invitations to that noble directness so characteristic of the Apostle to the Gentiles? The greater the difficulty, the clearer the call to proclaim Christ and Him crucified.

APRIL 10

And behold, there was a man named Joseph (LUKE 23:50).

There had to be such a man at just that time and place, because of one little detail in Isaiah's wonderful fifty-third chapter: "he made his grave with the wicked, and with the rich in his death" (v. 9). And God saw to the fulfillment of that detail by leading Joseph of Arimathea, a rich man, to come and take charge of Jesus' body. Let us not think the incident unimportant. All four evangelists record it. May not this fourfold emphasis on our Lord's entombment be intended to remind us that He not only suffered but also tasted death for us? Yes, the burial of Jesus is essential to the Gospel. No cross—no death and burial; no burial—no resurrection; no resurrection—no newness of life in Christ.

APRIL 11

But the just shall live by his faith (HABAKKUK 2:4).

The Apostle Paul, under the Spirit's guidance, took these words and built upon them the great epistle to the Romans. Augustine, Luther, Wesley, and others came into touch with this truth as set forth in Romans; and when they did, great things happened.

Has this truth found you? Do you know, beyond a shadow of a doubt, that you are justified by faith in the crucified and risen Christ, that you are accepted as righteous by God, that your sins are forgiven, that you are saved, and that all this is through the grace of God in Christ, who died and rose for you? If you do, you can never be the same person you were before this message gripped your life. What a message it is! No wonder Paul wrote these inspiring words, "I am not ashamed of the gospel of Christ, for it is the power of God unto salvation to everyone that believeth" (Romans 1:16).

APRIL 12

But upon Mount Zion shall be deliverance, and there shall be holiness. . . . and the kingdom shall be the Lord's (OBADIAH 17, 21).

At the close of his brief prophecy, Obadiah looks forward to the coming kingdom. In doing so he states one of the great reasons why the expectation of establishing that kingdom only by human efforts is a delusion. "There shall," he writes, "be holiness." So an essential element of God's kingdom is holiness. But that is something that we, apart from the Lord, simply do not possess. The kingdom, therefore, can only be consummated through the coming King, for He alone is perfectly holy. Let us then "wait for the blessed hope—the glorious appearing of our great God and Saviour, Jesus Christ" (Titus 2:13, NIV), and let us do so not passively but in an expectancy that serves Christ in full discipleship here and now, for "he gave himself for us to redeem us from all wickedness and to purify for himself a people that are his very own, eager to do what is good" (Titus 2:14, NIV).

APRIL 13

But he answered and said, It is written, Man shall not live by bread alone, but by every word that proceedeth out of the mouth of God (MATTHEW 4:4).

Our Lord refused to make an exception of Himself. To be sure, He was unique. Of all who ever lived on earth, He only was the God-Man. But though He was God manifest in the flesh, He was also truly human. He met the tempter upon the battleground of our common humanity, where you and I face the enemy. And meeting him there, He conquered.

What an advantage the devil took in directing his first temptation at Jesus' body! Weakened through fasting forty days and nights, it was crying out for food. And Jesus could indeed have turned the stones into bread to satisfy His great need. But that resort to the exceptional would have been a hindrance rather than a help to us sinners. So in gracious humility, our Lord took the hard way. He remained hungry for our sakes, and overcame this first temptation by quoting, as He did in the other two temptations, the Word of God from Deuteronomy. Thus He showed us tne way to victory over the enemy of our souls. For we too have access to God's Word and we also can use it to resist the tempter's assaults against us.

APRIL 14

To thee I lift up my eyes, O thou who art enthroned in the heavens! Behold, as the eyes of servants look to the hand of their master, as the eyes of a maid to the hand of her mistress, so our eyes look to the Lord our God (PSALM 123:1, 2, RSV).

In these Songs of Ascents (Psalms 120-134), the writer repeats a word and then builds on it. Here the word "eyes" is repeated four times. The psalmist is showing us the ideal way to look to our Lord. The figure pictures loyal servants looking to their master. Their eyes are fixed upon his hand. They follow his every gesture and whenever he beckons they rise up to serve. It is a moving portrayal of the obedient humility that ought always to mark Christian living.

Some may not like the comparison. They have no interest in anything that savors of servitude. How misguided! None of us is great enough to take any place before Him who is enthroned in the heavens, but that of a humble servant, dependent wholly upon the Master's will.

APRIL 15

The dead praise not the Lord, neither any that go down into silence. But we will bless the Lord from this time forth and for evermore. Praise the Lord (PSALM 115:17, 18).

The Bible sets before us many signs of spiritual life Here is one of them. It is not an obscure sign, and if it is really in your life you will know it.

What is this sign? It is the sign of praise. "The dead," says the psalmist, "praise not the Lord." To be sure, he was probably referring to the physically dead. But in the light of New Testament truth this statement applies equally to the spiritually dead, those who are what Paul calls "dead in trespasses and sins." Such can never know the true meaning of praising God. Far different is it with the spiritually alive. Of them the Psalmist has written: "But we will bless the Lord, from this time forth and for evermore. Praise the Lord." True praise comes from a renewed heart and evidences new life in Christ.

APRIL 16

Remember Lot's wife (LUKE 17:32).

When Christ tells us to remember something, we do well to follow His instructions. His advice in this place carries us back to Genesis. Along with her husband, Lot's wife was delivered from Sodom by the sheer grace of God. Scripture tells us (Genesis 19:16) that the angels laid hold upon her hand as well as Lot's and brought her forth and set her outside the city. Lot finally learned his lesson. Once delivered from Sodom, he set his face toward the place where the Lord had brought him. Not so his wife. She looked back just once too often

Why should we remember this unfortunate woman? The context of our Lord's words tells us. These days are like those of Lot. As destruction menaced Sodom, so doom hangs over this present world. It is one thing to be delivered from temptation and sin by the grace of God. It is another thing, ha .ng been delivered, to keep on trifling with sin. The difference between Lot and his wife was great. The one, though weak and carnal, belonged in heart to God. The other, though a recipient of God's delivering grace, belonged in heart to Sodom. Lot's wife teaches us that hearts which continue to hold on to sin will not escape God's judgment.

APRIL 17

Caleb the son of Jephunneh; he shall see it, and to him will I give the land that he hath trodden upon, and to his children, because he hath wholly followed the Lord (DEUTE-RONOMY 1:36).

Think of living so as to have God say to you, "He has wholly followed me!" Why, just to have the Lord acknowledge that we have followed Him is glorious. But to have the God who never lies say, "He has wholly followed me," is perhaps the greatest distinction that can come to any man.

One thing is certain. This would never have been said of Caleb had he not lived each day in full dependence upon God. There is little use in making resolutions for complete obedience in the future. The only practical path to a life like Caleb's is through moment by moment obedience. Oh, to be able to say each evening: "Today I wholly followed the Lord!"

APRIL 18

Now when they saw the boldness of Peter and John, and perceived that they were unlearned and ignorant men, they marvelled; and they took knowledge of them, that they had been with Jesus (ACTS 4:13).

Companionship always leaves some mark upon us, depending on who our companions are and the time we spend with them. The hostile Sanhedrin, the Supreme Court of the Jews, could not fail to recognize with whom Peter and John had been. The thing that impressed them was the contrast between what these disciples were in themselves ("unlearned and ignorant men") and what they had become in Christ ("their boldness"). And the Sanhedrin could account for the change in no other way than companionship with Jesus.

Let us be more with our Lord. To spend time alone with Him in prayer and reading the Word and to worship Him in the fellowship of the Church are essential. But to serve others in His Name is also to be with Jesus, and it too leaves its mark on our lives.

APRIL 19

Reckon it nothing but joy, my brethren, whenever you find yourselves surrounded by various temptations (JAMES 1:2, Weymouth).

This is an amazing statement. Nobody would naturally do what James suggests, for nobody rejoices by himself in temptation or affliction.

Notice how completely inclusive James's exhortation is. He speaks of our being "surrounded by various temptations." He goes further than saying that we should rejoice; he says we are to count our situation "nothing but joy." In other words, he is telling us that the clouds not only have a silver lining, but that for us they may be transmuted into silver.

Only those who are assured that the power of God is on their side can look at affliction in this way. It would almost seem as if James were telling us to find our highest and fullest joy at our hardest times. This is indeed the victorious life—to "reckon it nothing but joy" when we are "surrounded by various temptations."

APRIL 20

Peace I leave with you, my peace I give unto you: not as the world giveth, give I unto you. Let not your heart be troubled, neither let it be afraid (JOHN 14:27).

Let us turn to the Greek New Testament to think through this familiar and ever beautiful passage. We do this in order to search deeper into the rich meaning of our Lord's words. What, then, does our Greek New Testament teach us about this verse? Its lesson is one of emphasis; the original sentence uses for "my" an emphatic form of the pronoun, and in the latter part of the verse the emphatic *ego* is used for "I". Perhaps we may best bring out the emphasis by printing the verse like this: "Peace I leave with you, *my* peace I give unto you: not as the world giveth, give *I* unto you."

Yes, the message of these pronouns is one of emphasis. It is not peace in general that the Lord Jesus has promised His disciples, but a very special peace, even His own peace that passes understanding. No spiritual treasure is more precious than that peace. May we accept it as our heritage today.

APRIL 21

I appeal to you for my son Onesimus. . . . Formerly he was
useless to you, but now he has become useful both to you
and me (PHILEMON 10, 11, NIV).

Paul had the sensitiveness of a true gentleman. Onesimus,
on whose behalf he wrote this little letter, was a runaway thief.
But with delicacy Paul refrains from using the bald term for
the sin of Onesimus. Rather does he simply call him "formerly
. . . useless," making an affectionate pun on his name, for
Onesimus means "useful." Every Christian should have the
kind of tact Paul displays here. The way we speak of the short-
comings of others reveals the quality of our own spirit. For
"tact," as someone has said, "is the antennae of the soul." And
these antennae are sensitive to anything that needlessly wounds
our neighbor for whom Christ died.

APRIL 22

But as for you, ye thought evil against me: but God meant
it unto good, to bring to pass, as it is this day, to save
much people alive (GENESIS 50:20).

This is the epilogue of the story of Joseph. His brethren had
deliberately tried to destroy him. Failing that, they sold him
into alien hands, broke their father's heart by reporting his
death, and thought they were rid of their brother for good. As
Joseph underwent trial and imprisonment in Egypt, all must
have seemed hopeless. But he lived to see the day when the
other side of the tapestry was revealed. Then he saw how great
God really is. His brothers had planned evil against Joseph. But
what they meant for evil God worked out for good in the life
of a man who truly loved Him.

Think of the supreme crime of the ages. Wicked men insti-
gated and carried out the crucifixion of Christ. But God overruled this greatest of crimes so as to turn it into the greatest of
blessings. Indeed nothing can happen to a believer beyond the
power of God to bend it to ultimate good. We might well write
over the whole story of Joseph the great principle—"All things
work together for good to them that love God, to them who are
the called according to his purpose" (Romans 8:28).

APRIL 23

The Lord is my rock, and my fortress, and my deliverer;
my God, my strength, in whom I will trust; my buckler,
and the horn of my salvation, and my high tower (PSALM
18:2).

Eight times in this sentence David uses the word "my," as he
describes his Lord in eight different ways. One does not have
to search farther for the secret of David's greatness. Here it is.
He was great because he had a great personal hold on God.
Philosophical and theological distinctions about the Deity can
by themselves never satisfy the heart that hungers and thirsts
after God. Only David-like faith, a personal hold upon the Almighty, can sustain us in this world. Paul had it. Peter had it.
So did John. Thomas the doubter came to it when he said, "My
Lord and my God." Oh, how we need that all-important, personal hold upon our Lord!

APRIL 24

Suddenly there shone from heaven a great light round
about me. And I fell unto the ground, and heard a voice
saying unto me, Saul, Saul, why persecutest thou me?
(ACTS 22:6, 7).

The book of Acts contains three accounts of Paul's conversion. The first is that by Luke, as he records the event in the
ninth chapter. The next is this one which occurs in Paul's defense before the hostile mob in Jerusalem. And the last is in the
twenty-sixth chapter where the Apostle speaks for himself before King Agrippa. The variations between these accounts are
the fluctuations that authenticate different reports of the same
event.

Humanly speaking, it was unlikely that Saul of Tarsus would
ever be converted. Of all prospects for conversion, he was
one of the most unpromising. But God looked with favor upon
him and brought him to a saving knowledge of His Son. God's
thoughts are not our thoughts, or His ways our ways.
How marvelous that He took the arch-persecutor of the first
Christians and made him the greatest missionary of the cross
the world has ever known! Surely none of us need ever be discouraged, as we throw ourselves upon the mercy of the Lord.
Those who go to Him for refuge will find that His promise—
"him that cometh to me I will in no wise cast out" (John 6:37b)
—is wonderfully true.

APRIL 25

Beloved, let us love one another. . . . He who does not love does not know God; for God is love (1 JOHN 4:7a, 8, RSV).

This is John's unforgettable way of asserting the primacy of love. Like so many of his sayings, it is very simple and at the same time very deep. Reduced to its simplest terms it amounts to this: no love, no God. No amount of wisdom, or strength, or any other virtue can ever take the place of love. One may be a Christian and lack many things, but love for others is an essential part of knowing God. Oh, to have each of our actions and human relationships today rooted and grounded in the love of Christ!

APRIL 26

Demas hath forsaken me, having loved this present world (2 TIMOTHY 4:10a).

A tragic epitaph on a Christian life! Demas was privileged as few men; he had the honor of being in personal fellowship with the great Apostle to the Gentiles. By the simple virtue of faithfulness he might have had a distinguished ministry. But he sold the undying praise of God for idolatrous occupation with the world. He exchanged the company of the prisoner of the Lord for the trinkets of sin.

There is a lesson in Demas's failure. For one thing, it shows us that fellowship with even the greatest saint is not enough to keep the erring heart from sin. Belonging to a church where a true man of God is pastor, sitting under a great Bible teacher —these are privileges but nothing more. We do not go to heaven through another's faith, nor do we keep our testimony vital through the sanctity of others. Only full commitment to the Lord Jesus can deliver us from Demas's kind of tragedy.

APRIL 27

Therefore choose life (DEUTERONOMY 30:19b).

This is what God always wants men to choose. As He says through Moses in this very same chapter, "I have set before thee this day life and good, and death and evil" (v. 15). Yes, man has a choice, and it is God's desire for man to choose rightly. But where is there true life unless in Christ? "In him was life: and the life was the light of men" (John 1:4).

Have you who are reading these words chosen Christ? Have you, by a definite act of your will, turned away from all trust in self-righteousness and personal merit, and put your faith in Him as your only Saviour? For every one who comes to Him Christ *is* life. To choose Him as Lord and Saviour is to have life everlasting. To refuse Him means eternal death through everlasting separation from God. Said the Lord Jesus to those who were rejecting Him, "And ye will not come to me, that ye might have life" (John 5:40). May He never say that of any who are reading this message today!

APRIL 28

Now Daniel determined not to contaminate himself by touching the food and wine assigned him by the king, and he begged the master of the eunuchs not to make him do so (DANIEL 1:8, NEB).

Among the young men of Judah taken into captivity, those of highest promise were chosen for special training in Nebuchadnezzar's own palace. But only Daniel, Hananiah, Mishael, and Azariah are remembered. The reason is that these four, with Daniel as their spokesman, had the moral courage to be nonconformists in the king's palace (Daniel 1:6-21).

What far-reaching influence a single act of moral courage has! And what a difficult decision faced Daniel and his companions! Why, the king's food represented the very best great Babylon had to offer. But Daniel had the discernment to realize that even the world's best may defile the Lord's children. So, supported by his three faithful companions, he stood his ground, with the result that the book bearing his name stands as a witness to the blessing flowing from the courage of a young man in the palace of an alien monarch.

APRIL 29

And Ruth said, Intreat me not to leave thee, or to return from following after thee: for whither thou goest, I will go; and where thou lodgest, I will lodge: thy people shall be my people, and thy God my God: Where thou diest, will I die, and there will I be buried: the Lord do so to me, and more also, if ought but death part thee and me (RU H 1:16, 17).

This is one of the most beautiful utterances ever to fall from human lips. It needs to be read aloud for its lovely cadences to be fully appreciated.

We may well take Ruth's words as a model for our soul's relationship to Christ. For we shall be better Christians if we have more of her fidelity. Ruth never once says that she loves Naomi; she just proves it beyond a shadow of a doubt by her intense desire to follow her mother-in-law even to death. One of the truest tests of love is desire to be with the beloved. Would that we had a similar longing for constant companionship with our Lord Jesus!

APRIL 30

While he yet spake, behold, a bright cloud overshadowed them: and behold a voice of the cloud, which said, This is my beloved Son, in whom I am well pleased; hear ye him (MATTHEW 17:5).

Have you ever considered the paradox of the "bright cloud"? Usually we think of clouds as dark. Coming between us and the sun, they shut out the light. The lear sky speaks of serenity and joy; the cloudy sky typifies sorrow and trouble. But this cloud of the transfiguration was bright. Why? Well, God was behind it, for He spoke out of it and said, "This is my beloved Son, in whom I am well pleased; hear ye him."

So we consider an application to our lives. When clouds of tribulation come in our experience, as they surely will, let us remember that every Christian is in the hands of the Sovereign God. Therefore, we may know that the Almighty is shining behind every cloud in our lives and that through them He has something to say to us about His dear Son.

MAY 1

So then they that are in the flesh cannot please God (ROMANS 8:8).

We must make our choice. To live after the flesh is to live the purely human life, which is the self-life. (As someone said of this Pauline term "flesh," if you take off the "h" and spell it backwards, you have its meaning.) Now if we insist on living after the flesh, there are many things we may do and many heights to which we may attain. We may make money, gain social prestige, win political prominence, or reach artistic and literary heights. But if we are living after the flesh and only after the flesh, of this one thing we may be certain: *We cannot please God.* It is folly to minimize the scope of activity open to the flesh. And it is also folly to think that the self-life can ever please God. The choice is between the praise of men and the praise of God. Let wealth and fame come, as sometimes they do, but let our aim be first of all the will of God.

MAY 2

Behold, I have made thy face strong against their faces, and thy forehead strong against their foreheads. As an adamant harder than flint have I made thy forehead: fear them not, neither be dismayed at their looks, though they be a rebellious house (EZEKIEL 3:8-9).

This is how God fortified Ezekiel for the trying task of denouncing his own people. It strikes at the heart of one of the hardest things any man may be called upon to endure. "Fear them not, neither be dismayed at their looks." There is indeed an awful power in the hostile look. The eye can express hatred or ridicule that a sensitive person finds cruel and hard to face. It was for this test of the contemptuous gaze that God was preparing Ezekiel. He promised to make the prophet's forehead as impervious as flint, so that he would be strong against the stares of his enemies. The armor of God is a complete armor. When a man is doing His will, nothing—neither scornful look, nor scathing word, nor wicked deed—can hold him from his appointed task.

MAY 3

Come, and let us smite him with the tongue (JEREMIAH
18: 18b).

From the physical point of view the threat is ridiculous. A
man would be hard put to kill a fly with his tongue. But actually that threat of Jeremiah's enemies expressed a terribly real
danger. With the tongue a career may be smashed, a reputation
blasted as by a charge of high explosive, a life withered, shriv-
elled, and finally killed. God forbid that a Christian tongue
should ever do such evil things! O believer, place your
tongue in your Lord's keeping. Ask Him to bridle it that you
may not smite some other person and do him injury with your
tongue.

MAY 4

*Then they said one to another, We do not well: this day
is a day of good tidings, and we hold our peace: if we tarry
till the morning light, some mischief will come upon us:
now therefore come, that we may go and tell the king's
household* (2 KINGS 7 9).

Samaria, besieged by the Syrians, was in a state of acute
famine. Four lepers were at its gate. They had their choice of
entering the city to die of famine or of going to the Syrian camp
with the hope of finding food. They chose the latter and were
amazed to find the camp deserted. The Lord had put the enemy
to flight.

First the lepers ate and drank. Then one of them spoke up
and said, "We do not well: this day is a day of good tidings,
and we hold our peace." So they returned to Samaria with the
good news that the Syrians had fled, leaving all their possessions in the camp.

So with us sinners saved by grace. We have an obligation to
do as those humble lepers. If by the grace of God we who know
the Gospel can say, "This day is a day of good tidings," then
how can we fail to bring to the spiritually starving the good
news about Christ, who is the living Bread?

MAY 5

Now the eyes of Israel were dim for age, so that he could not see. And he brought them near unto him; and he kissed them, and embraced them (GENESIS 48:10).

Jacob closes his life with a scene similar but also very different from that when his father Isaac died. Isaac, too, was dim of sight when on his death bed, but Jacob took advantage of his father's affliction and obtained the blessing by deceit. How gracious God was! Now that Jacob himself was blind, he was not treated as he had treated his father. Rather he was accorded all love and respect. With deep deference, Joseph brought his two boys before the aged patriarch. To be sure, Jacob preferred Ephraim to Manasseh (v. 20), but this was clearly of God and stands as an example of the overruling principle of election, which He exercised at Jacob's own birth (Romans 9:10-13). The God who was so kind to Jacob deals graciously with his own today. None of us merits His favor; all we have and are is of God's unpurchasable love in Christ.

MAY 6

But will God indeed dwell on the earth? Behold, heaven and the highest heaven cannot contain thee; how much less this house which I have built? (I KINGS 8:27, RSV).

The estimate of God revealed in Solomon's prayer of dedication answers the popular misconception that claims that the Old Testament portrays a mere tribal god whom the Israelites considered their private deity. It is supposed that this tribal deity developed under the religious insight of the later prophets till he finally reached New Testament status. But here, in this noble prayer dedicating the temple, Solomon speaks of God in the most exalted, universal terms. No prophet reveals a wider conception of Jehovah than does Solomon in these glorious phrases.

The presupposition that the Christian religion has evolved is not just unhistorical. Spiritually, it is perilous and leads to the blasphemy that God is made in man's image. No, the God of the Old Testament is no invention of the Hebrews. He is the transcendent Lord of heaven and earth. He is the Father of our Lord Jesus Christ. So let us rejoice in His greatness as we serve Him today.

MAY 7

I have given them thy word (JOHN 17:14a).

At this point in His high-priestly prayer the Lord Jesus refers to His great gift to His Church. He has given them God's Word. How has He done that? Well, first of all He has given it to them through a perfect example. He alone is the incarnate Word; He alone fulfilled all righteousness; He alone is the flawless living epistle. Again, He has given God's written Word a new meaning. The days of His life on earth shed new light upon the Word. His work on Calvary illuminates all Scripture with a light that will never die. So He has given His Church the Word in its fullness of meaning. Finally, He has given His own the Word in power, even the power of His resurrection that works in us by faith. Yes, He has given us God's Word. Have you received it, because you have received Him?

MAY 8

Felix arrived. . . . He sent for Paul and listened to him as he spoke about faith in Christ Jesus. As Paul discoursed on righteousness, self-control and the judgment to come, Felix was afraid . . . (ACTS 24:24, 25, NIV).

These two sentences give us an excellent insight into what makes Christian preaching powerful. The first states that Paul spoke about faith in Christ. The second shows how he directed his message straight at the personal life of Felix. Today there are many men and women like Felix. They can listen unmoved and even with enjoyment to lofty spiritual teaching. But when that teaching gets down to their unrighteousness and their lack of self-control and the judgment they must face, it's another story. Then they tremble. It is well to remember that it is not always the message bringing the loudest "Amens" that God uses the most. In this instance, Paul clearly shows us that reasoning about moral and ethical questions has an integral relation to the Gospel proclamation.

MAY 9

So be it, O Lord (JEREMIAH 11·5b).

These few words characterize one of the greatest of God's prophets. A man of tender heart, living in an evil day, called to prophesy doom to an apostate people, Jeremiah suffered as few men have ever suffered. But not once was he unfaithful in courageously proclaiming the whole Word of God. The key to his character is found in the words, "So be it, O Lord." Jeremiah, in his own life the most Christ-like of the prophets, was committed to absolute obedience to God. "So be it, O Lord." When we learn to say that in every circumstance, we are on the way to godly living.

MAY 10

And an highway shall be there, and a way, and it shall be called The way of holiness; the unclean shall not pass over it; but it shall be for those: the wayfaring men, though fools, shall not err therein (ISAIAH 35:8).

Not forgetting the original application of these words to Israel, the Christian reader rejoices in their implications. What a beautiful picture they present of the clarity of the way of salvation! Think of "the way of holiness" of which Isaiah speaks as the path through Christ to God. That road is for the "wayfaring man"; it is for every pilgrim such as you and me. So plain is that way that even pilgrims of little discernment (Isaiah uses the word "fools") shall not mistake it. There is only one qualification for traveling that path to its blessed end; it is that of being cleansed. And God has freely met that qualification for us in the precious blood of the Son. There are many difficult things in the Bible, and this book of Isaiah contains some of them; but the most important things, those on which our souls' destiny depends, are plain. "The way of holiness" is as clear as John 3:16, John 14:6, Romans 10:9,10, and the other great Gospel texts. Are your feet planted firmly on it? Are you in the Way that is Christ?

MAY 11

But when Peter was come to Antioch, I withstood him to the face, because he was to be blamed (GALATIANS 2:11).

This revealing verse shows us Paul's moral courage. For a comparative newcomer into the fellowship of the apostles to blame openly one of the original twelve was an audacious act. But Paul was utterly committed to the defense of the Gospel. The man who wrote that anyone must be accursed, even "an angel from heaven," who preached any other Gospel than the one that had been revealed to him (Galations 1:8), was not to be overawed by Peter.

In this day of doctrinal compromise we need more of Paul's oyalty to the one Faith. May we never confuse sentimentality with the love of Christ, nor tolerance with being afraid to speak up for the truth.

MAY 12

I am my beloved's, and my beloved is mine (SONG OF SOLOMON 6:3a).

The bride is speaking of the bridegroom. Her words are simple, but their meaning profound. "I am my beloved's." We can understand this. Every mature man or woman who has experienced human love can to some degree enter into the meaning of these words. Spiritually they symbolize the wholesouled surrender to the Lord, the union with Him, that is at the heart of Christian living.

"And my beloved is mine." This is still more wonderful. Because we can yield ourselves to Christ, we can appreciate the bride's first word. But to be able to say of Him, "And my Beloved is mine"—that is far different. Think of it; The Saviour, the Lord of glory, our blessed Lord Jesus Christ, condescends to love us with such a love that we, the unworthy recipients of it may dare to say of Him, "My beloved is mine."

MAY 13

Children, obey your parents in the Lord: for this is right (EPHESIANS 6:1).

Scripture speaks directly to all sorts and conditions of men. Here is a word given expressly for young Christians. Young man or woman, boy or girl, you who know Christ as Saviour, are you following this advice? You may be certain of this. No amount of spiritual experience or testimony or service can make up either for deliberate or thoughtless disobedience to your Christian parents. And fathers and mothers, are you dealing with your children with the loving firmness that builds them up in obedience and in respect?

MAY 14

And he said unto me, My grace is sufficient for thee: for my strength is made perfect in weakness (2 CORINTHIANS 12:9a).

This comforting word came, as the context shows, out of Paul's deep personal trial. No one can tell with certainty exactly what Paul's thorn in the flesh was. And it is just as well that we do not know, for this very doubt about the identity of Paul's trial gives his experience universal relevance for troubled souls.

The initial verb "said" is in the perfect tense. Dean Alford commented in his *Greek Testament* that here the full meaning cannot be represented in English by the verb alone. He suggested this paraphrase: "He said, and that answer is enough." When we come to God in our extremity, He gives us His answer, and His answer is enough.

And what answer was given Paul? It was the great word regarding the all-sufficiency of divine grace. Notice the very personal way in which that grace is described. It is not grace in general that the Lord promised Paul. It is *"my* grace." Grace in general is merely favor; "my grace," in the sense of the grace of the Lord Jesus Christ, is the precious gift He gives His own.

MAY 15

For no matter how many promises God has made, they are "Yes" in Christ. And so through him the "Amen" is spoken by us to the glory of God (2 CORINTHIANS 1:20, NIV).

What a tribute to Christ! It presents Him as the great Fulfiller of the divine promises. He is the living Affirmative; in Him every heavenly pledge is fully endorsed. If we are able to say "Amen" ("So be it") to any Scripture promise given us from Genesis to Revelation, it is only because Christ by His divine "Yes" has guaranteed its fulfillment. Why, then, should we have the least doubt as to even one of the divine promises? God has spoken them; Christ has confirmed them; we must believe them.

MAY 16

Bezalel the son of Uri, son of Hur, of the tribe of Judah, made all that the Lord commanded Moses (EXODUS 38:22, RSV).

In the account of the construction of the tabernacle the name of Bezalel is prominent. In chapter thirty-five, we are told that the Lord had "filled him with the Spirit of God, in wisdom, in understanding, and in knowledge, and in all manner of workmanship" (v. 31). And in the same place we are told that Bezalel had a helper, named Oholiab, and that both Bezalel and Oholiab were favored of God with the gift of teaching as well as craftsmanship. Bezalel used his God-given skill in working with his hands and in teaching his art to others for the glory of God. God used his talent as an instrument with which the tabernacle, with its symbolism of the coming Messiah and Redeemer, was constructed. Every Christian, humble though his gift may be, may take encouragement from what God did through a consecrated workman like Bezalel. "Make me a Bezalel, O Lord," may well be our prayer.

MAY 17

One generation shall praise thy works to another, and shall declare thy mighty acts (PSALM 145:4).

Some ecclesiastical authorities speak of apostolic succession, but here is a greater succession. Think of it! Down through the ages men have been praising God and declaring His mighty acts. This succession did not originate at Rome; it began in Eden. It is not handed down from bishop to bishop, but from father to son, from mother to daughter, from friend to friend, from believer to believer. All the way from Adam to us there has been this never-ending chain of praise. Are you participating in it? No Christian life is complete that does not join in this unending succession of praise to the living God.

MAY 18

She has been a helper of many and of myself as well (RO-MANS 16:2, RSV).

Paul is speaking of Phoebe, the Christian woman from the church at Cenchreae, whom he used to bring his greatest epistle to the church at Rome. It is a beautiful recommendation he gives her—that she helped him and many others. Aside from this little reference at the close of Romans, we know nothing of Phoebe. But what a tribute to her Christian life and what worldwide recognition the generous pen of the Apostle has bestowed on her!

None of us has the spiritual stature of a Paul. But we may all do what Phoebe did. We may be known for the Christian virtue of helpfulness. The opportunity to exercise this virtue is always at hand. We are all surrounded by others. Friends, relatives, acquaintances afford plenty of chances for true helpfulness. There may be among us some Christian to whom we may be of special help. Not every believer may enter the ministry or go to the mission field, but all may follow in the noble succession of Phoebe.

MAY 19

*The priest shall burn all on the altar, to be a burnt sacri-
fice. . . . And if his offering be of the flocks . . . he shall
bring it a male without blemish* (LEVITICUS 1:9,10).

This burnt offering, which comes first in Leviticus, typifies
the perfect work of Christ. It was completely consumed; unlike
certain other sacrifices, no portion of it was to be eaten. The
altar on which it was laid had burning on it a perpetual fire.
The whole thing speaks of the Lord Jesus who was fully devoted
to His Father's will. Just as all His life and ministry was well
pleasing to God, so the whole of the burnt-offering rose "a sweet
savour unto the Lord" (v. 9).

The great phrase in Leviticus is "holiness unto the Lord."
And here at the very opening of the book there is exhibited the
secret of holiness. Christ was holy because He was completely
given over to God. And as it is with the Master, so must it be
with the servants. The extent of our holiness is always the
extent of our yieldedness to God.

MAY 20

*"The Lord be a true and faithful witness between us, if we
do not even according to all things for which the Lord thy
God shall send thee to us* (JEREMIAH 42:5).

This is what the leaders of the people said to Jeremiah. They
had inquired what the Word of God from Jeremiah was and
had promised to do it. And the plain statement of God's will
came through the prophet. In clearest terms they were warned
against going to Egypt. Yet the very next chapter tells us that
they straightway went down to Egypt.

What they did is all too characteristic of some of us. We
pray for guidance. God answers us. And then we disobey Him,
because all along we have been determined to go our own way.
Let us not pray for God's guidance, unless we are willing at all
costs to do what He tells us to do.

MAY 21

The common faith (Trrus 1:4).

Let us thank God that the greatest things in life are common, available for all. All may share the basic experiences of love, joy, sorrow, and the like. And the greatest of all blessings, the Christian faith, is also common. The Gospel knows no aristocracy.

In respect to salvation there is no "forgotten man." God would have all to be saved. Whoever will, may take the water of life freely. To refuse, then, to share the Gospel, to be disinterested ın bringing the message of salvation to the unevangelized, to regard the good news as private spiritual property, is a perversion of the very purpose of God. The "common faith" must go to all men and you and I must do our utmost to see that it gets there.

MAY 22

Thus I have looked for thee in the sanctuary, that I might behold thy power and glory (Psalm 63:2, Psalter, Book of Common Prayer.)

Not everyone knows where to look for the power and glory of the Lord. Some would see His greatness in the rise and fall of nations. Others would behold Him in the beauty of nature. And it is true that in these and in other places He manifests His greatness.

But there is another and more accessible place to behold His power and glory. That is, as the psalmist tells us, the sanctuary. For the ancient Hebrew, the sanctuary was in the tabernacle and later in the temple. For Christians it varies greatly, being for some a church or cathedral, for others a humble chapel, a neighborhood meeting, a family prayer circle, or an individual quiet time. So the sanctuary is the place of worship wherever it may be.

Ours is an age of violent power. But really to know the power and glory of the Lord we must turn from the spectacular to the spiritual. It is in worship that God's glory is best seen. Ezekiel by the river Chebar saw a sublime vision of God. Isaiah beheld the Lord high and lifted up in the temple. John on Patmos saw the Lord in glory. If we would know more of the greatness of our God, let us spend more time in worship.

MAY 23

The Lord's Day (REVELATION 1:10).

Emphasize the possessive case of the noun and you have the essence of the Christian's day of worship. It is the *Lord's* Day. Therefore, it belongs peculiarly to Him and, because it belongs to Him, it must be commemorated by honoring His Name. As a Christian you have liberty to do or not to do this. It is not the calendar that will make Sunday the Lord's Day for you; it is you yourself. By going to public worship, by taking extra time for your Bible and for prayer, by thinking about the things that are true, honest, just, pure, lovely, and of good report, you can make Sunday a hallowed day. But spend its hours only on newspapers, overeating, sports, or social activities, and, whatever your calendar says, it is for you just Self Day and not the Lord's Day.

MAY 24

And Judah said unto his brethren, What profit is it if we slay our brother, and conceal his blood? Come, and let us sell him to the Ishmaelites, and let not our hand be upon him; for he is our brother and our flesh. And his brethren were content (GENESIS 37:26, 27).

"His brethren were content." Content with what? That is the question. Here were nine brothers perfectly satisfied with an atrocious piece of deception. They were quite happy to sell their younger brother into captivity and to perpetrate a ghastly subterfuge upon their aged father. The most deplorable thing that can be said of them is expressed in these five words: "And his brethren were content."

But Judah and Simeon and all the others were not unique in this unholy contentment. All of us, yes, all of us Christians, have at one time or another been in their position. We too have been content with sin. We have even been content with the rejection of the only begotten Son of God. But God in His grace has brought us to a conviction of our sin so that, no longer content, we have been turned from unbelief to faith. Then let us be very careful never to lapse into a state of satisfaction with any kind of evil.

MAY 25

And the children of Israel did according to all that the Lord commanded Moses: so they [encamped] by their standards, and so they set forward, everyone after their families, according to the house of their fathers (NUMBERS 2:34).

These early chapters of Numbers are packed with details. Name after name of obscure persons is mentioned. Enumerations of tribes and families follow one another in precise order. This all illustrates the obedience of Moses and also that of Israel. Moses transmitted the command of God; it remained for the people to obey.

Sometimes we Christians long for clearer and more detailed guidance. But such a relationship to God entails special responsibilities. Explicit guidance means explicit obedience. If we seek God's leading in everything, we must be willing to do everything He asks us. When we receive God's instructions, we may not pick and choose which ones we obey. Our obligation is to be like the children of Israel at this place in their experience and to do "according to all that the Lord commanded."

MAY 26

As Christ was raised up from the dead by the glory of the Father, even so we also should walk in newness of life (ROMANS 6:4).

Only Christians can respond to this appeal. But to them how powerful it is! "We . . . should 'walk about' [for so the verb may be translated] in newness of life," writes Paul. He is beginning some of the most profound teaching in his epistles, the section of Romans that deals with sanctification. But, as is the case with the deep things of God, its basis is simple. Do Christians possess new life in Christ? Then let them walk in it. The new life in our risen Lord is not given us just to be discussed and talked about; it is given us to be lived. Salvation is pardon from the guilt and future penalty of sin. But it is also more than that; as a new life, it is to be enjoyed here and now. And the way to enjoy that life is to walk about in it while constantly looking unto Jesus.

MAY 27

Praying always with all prayer and supplication (EPHE-
SIANS 6:18a).

It is a mistake to divorce this verse from the preceding description (vv. 11-17) of the whole armor of God and the
sword of the Spirit. For it emphasizes another thing that is essential to successful spiritual combat. Constant prayer, always,
and at all times—that is the strategy the Christian soldier must
follow. Completely protected and equipped with his spiritual
sword, he may yet be as lifeless and powerless as an armored
statue. Prayer is not just desirable; it is essential. It is the channel
whereby God's omnipotent power flows into human life. It
turns nominal Christians into victorious spiritual warriors.

MAY 28

*Howbeit I believed not the words, until I came, and mine
eyes had seen it: and, behold, the half was not told me: thy
wisdom and prosperity exceedeth the fame which I heard*
(1 KINGS 10:7).

It is the Queen of Sheba speaking. Having seen Solomon in
all his magnificence, this is her testimony. You and I can never
see the greatness of Solomon's kingdom. We can only read
about his wisdom, his wealth, the beauty of his palace, and the
glory of the temple he built. Yet we have before us a far greater
prospect than what the Queen of Sheba looked forward to on
her journey to Jerusalem. One day we shall see the Greater
than Solomon. We shall behold the King in all His risen
splendor. We shall see Christ face to face. The Bible tells us
wonderful things about heaven and the glory of the Lamb. But
when at last we see Him, as we surely shall, then like Sheba's
Queen we too shall say, "The half was not told me." It is a
wonderful thing to be a Christian, if for no other reason than
the glorious future toward which every believer may look.

> *Face to face with Christ my Saviour,*
> *Face to face, how can it be?*
> *When with rapture I behold Him,*
> *Jesus Christ, who died for me.*

MAY 29

For they shall not be ashamed [disappointed] that wait for me (ISAIAH 49:23b).

There are occasions when we must wait for God. His time schedule is not ours. But though the waiting seems long, the outcome is certain. Nobody who bides God's time will ever be disappointed. The world may misunderstand and mock the patience of believers. Yet faith in the Lord who does all things well will ever find its ultimate justification. Therefore, keep on praying, Christian parent with a burden for your child's salvation or restoration. Keep on praying, Christian child, for your parents whom you long to see brought into the knowledge of Christ. Keep on praying, suffering believer with a thorn in the flesh nothing seems to help or with a sorrow you can hardly bear. God Himself has said, "They shall not be ashamed that wait for me." In His own time and in His own way He will act on your behalf in accordance with His perfect love.

MAY 30

Christ Jesus, who of God is made unto us wisdom, and righteousness, and sanctification, and redemption (1 CORINTHIANS 1:30).

"Wisdom, and righteousness, and sanctification, and redemption." These belong to us Christians. Christ came that they might be realized in our lives. They refer not only to the believer's position before God; they refer also to the believer's present experience. There is a present as well as a past tense of redemption. Sin besets us daily and we need deliverance. Christ's righteousness is imputed to us by faith and we need daily to realize that righteousness in our lives. He is the wisdom of God and He will also be our wisdom. Hour by hour we need to grow into a closer walk with Him. The great message of this verse is that God has already made Christ all these things for us. They are our present resources and are possessed when we commit ourselves wholly to Him.

MAY 31

He is brought as a lamb to the slaughter, and as a sheep before her shearers is dumb, so he openeth not his mouth (ISAIAH 53:7b).

If we remember of whom the prophet is speaking, we shall be the better able to appreciate the wonder of these words. As Christians know, this fifty-third chapter of Isaiah looks forward to the cross. Its subject from beginning to end is the Lord Jesus who atoned for our sin. Where the prophet writes that "He is brought as a lamb to the slaughter, and as a sheep before her shearers is dumb, so he openeth not his mouth," we may ask, "But who is He?" Well, He is none other than the One of whom David writes, "The Lord is my shepherd" (Psalm 23:1). He is the "great shepherd of the sheep," of whom we read at the close of the epistle to the Hebrews (13:20, 21). According to His own words, He is "The good shepherd who giveth his life for the sheep" (John 10:11). But Isaiah shows Him in the place of the sheep: "He is brought as a lamb to the slaughter, and as a sheep before her shearers is dumb, so he openeth not his mouth."

A strange reversal of position! The good Shepherd is Himself being led like a sheep to the place of death. How can this be? We who are saved by His grace know the answer. We know that our only hope of forgiveness and eternal life lies in the fact that He, the great Shepherd of the sheep, actually took our place. For us the Son of God voluntarily became the Lamb of God.

JUNE 1

Sing, O barren, thou that didst not bear; break forth into singing, and cry aloud, thou that didst not travail with child, for more are the children of the desolate than the children of the married wife, saith the Lord (ISAIAH 54:1).

As we saw yesterday the subject of the fifty-third chapter of Isaiah is the cross. A marvel of literature, this chapter gives the meaning of Calvary over seven hundred years before the event took place. But all too few who read Isaiah fifty-three go on to note the beginning of the fifty-fourth chapter. "Sing"! This is the word with which the prophet continues, for the experience of God's redeeming grace on Calvary brings a joyful song to the believer's heart.

A farmer whose land was traversed by a railroad put up a sign at the crossing. His sign was in two pieces, and this is how it read, "Cross-sing." What if he did put in an extra "s"? Unintentionally that farmer proclaimed a great message. We are redeemed through what Christ did for us on the cross (Isaiah 53). And then we rejoice because the Lord Himself puts a new song in our mouths (Psalm 40:3).

JUNE 2

And beyond question, the mystery of godliness is great; He appeared in a body . . . was believed on in the world, was taken up in glory (1 TIMOTHY 3:16, NIV).

Observe that Paul does not say that Christ is believed on by the world. The Bible never teaches world conversion but rather stresses the calling out of God's people from the world.

We need to remind ourselves that belief in the sense of complete personal trust is essential to godliness. Without trust in Jesus Christ no amount of knowledge of the Bible, theology, ethics, or any other related subject can by itself ever make us godly. The world will offer God almost anything but this one all-important element of belief. It will offer Him service and even praise of a sort. But it will never give Him belief. Belief is too humbling; it requires that one come to God as a little child. Yes, God wants those who are willing to take Him at His Word and believe implicitly in His Son, in His loving care, and in the full reliability of all His precious promises!

JUNE 3

His mother saith unto the servants, Whatsoever he saith unto you, do it (JOHN 2:5).

This advice is significant, because it comes from the person who knew the Lord Jesus best. Surely Mary was closer to Him through the greater part of His earthly life than any other human being. "Whatsoever he saith unto you, do it." Things would be different were every Christian consistently to follow those words. There is nothing ambiguous about them; they are crystal clear. And what a perfect rule for life they are! Whatever the Lord Jesus asks us to do, that we are to do. All who are living and walking in fellowship with Christ will concur in this advice of His mother. The nearer a believer is to his Lord, the more he realizes the necessity for obeying Him fully.

JUNE 4

And after Abimelech there arose to defend Israel Tola the son of Puah, the son of Dodo, a man of Issachar; and he dwelt in Shamir in Mount Ephraim. And he judged Israel twenty and three years, and died, and was buried in Shamir (JUDGES 10:1, 2).

This is all we know of Tola, the seventh judge. His name means "a worm"; and he stands in sharp contrast to Abimelech, the usurper who grasped for kingship. Abimelech brought ruin and bloodshed to the city of Shechem and destruction upon himself. Then God took the "worm," Tola, and used him for twenty-three years of peaceful administration over Israel.

Through the terse words of this record there gleams the bright hope of what God can do with the insignificant. In comparison with the great of this world most of us are little. According to men's opinion we are insignificant. But He who used a Tola can also use us. He can make us channels of peace and blessing to many. He can do through us works that will endure. There is no virtue in a humility that hides its head in inactivity. But there is power in a humility that, realizing its insignificance, dares to place itself expectantly at God's disposal. Even the humblest may be a Tola for Christ.

JUNE 5

If I may but touch his clothes, I shall be whole (MARK 5:28).

For twelve weary years the woman who said these words had suffered from a dreadful affliction. Then one day in a crowd she touched the Lord Jesus. To be sure, she knew little of Him Possibly she thought of Him somewhat superstitiously. But she did have faith in His ability to help her. And as she touched Him, she was healed.

Have you touched your Lord by faith today? Perhaps you are weary, or afflicted, or perplexed. Then reach out and touch Him by faith. Life's duties crowd upon you. Business or profession impose their many claims. Yet you have time for that touch, as your heart reaches out in faith to the Son of God.

> *We touch Him in life's throng and press,*
> *And we are whole again.*

JUNE 6

And I saw a great white throne, and him that sat on it, from whose face the earth and the heaven fled away; and there was found no place for them (REVELATION 20:11).

In the full meaning of a misused word, this is one of the most "awful" verses in the Bible. In a few phrases it gives a haunting picture of the terrible reckoning that awaits the lost. In that day of judgment there will be the great white throne with its mighty Occupant and the wicked dead, small and great, standing before Him. Then all human power will have vanished. Then ultimate justice will be administered.

As he looks at this picture, the Christian can but thank God that Christ saves to the uttermost. The great white throne is not a place before which any true child of God will stand. Those who have received Christ as Saviour have eternal life. For them the awful question of their everlasting destiny has been settled at the moment of their rebirth into the kingdom of God. Their names are already written in the book of life. But what believer can fail to be concerned about others, whether relatives, friends, neighbors, or the multitudes who have never heard of the Saviour? Callous and unloving is the Christian who has no burden for the lost and seldom prays for them.

JUNE 7

Take heed to your spirit (MALACHI 2:15b).

There are places in Scripture where false capitalization is a serious error. This is one of them. To capitalize "spirit" in this verse would make it refer to the Holy Spirit, whereas the context clearly implies that the human spirit is meant. So the warning is for every one of us. We all need daily to take heed to our own spirit. What a protean thing it is, this spirit of ours! At one moment it is loving, at another angry, at one moment compassionate, at another malicious. How it needs to be disciplined and held in check! Happy, therefore, is the Christian who knows how to take heed to his own spirit by letting the indwelling Holy Spirit have control of it.

JUNE 8

Go ye, inquire of the Lord for me, and for the people, and for all Judah, concerning the words of this book that is found: for great is the wrath of the Lord that is kindled against us, because our fathers have not hearkened unto the words of this book, to do according unto all that which is written concerning us (2 KINGS 22:13).

It was a great day in King Josiah's time when the law of Moses was found in the temple. The fact that it had been lost shows the low ebb of spiritual life in Judah. Here God's people were so backslidden that they had lost the Word of God and hardly missed it! But Hilkiah, the high priest, found the Pentateuch (in whole or in part and probably including Deuteronomy) somewhere in the temple. And when it was read before the king, he not only rent his clothes but he did more; he began and carried out one of the greatest reforms in Old Testament history. In Josiah's hands the lost book was powerful, because he recognized its application to himself and his people.

In those words Josiah had the key for the effective use of Scripture. He realized that it applied personally to king as well as people. Josiah is gone, but the book Hilkiah found and read to him remains. Let us never make the mistake of thinking that the Old Testament is only for the Jews. It relates to us also. Everywhere in Scripture we may find "that which is written concerning us." That is why we need to read the Word of God daily.

JUNE 9

And when he had looked round about on them with anger, being grieved for the hardness of their hearts, he saith unto the man, stretch forth thine hand (MARK 3:5).

These people were too religious to pity a poor, afflicted man. Ceremonial religion had dried up the milk of human kindness in them, and they placed legalistic Sabbath restrictions above the healing of the withered hand. Christ was angered and grieved "for the hardness of their hearts."

We Christian people should take note of some of the things that grieved our Lord, and remember that He is "the same yesterday, and today, and forever" (Hebrews 13:8). Was He grieved at the hardness of heart that could look at human suffering unmoved? Was He angered at religion that exercised its special privileges at the expense of the unfortunate and the afflicted? He is the same Christ today. No amount of orthodoxy can make up for the lack of concern for the needy that is obscuring the love of Christ in the lives of some of us respectable religious people in these times when many of us have so much while others have so little.

JUNE 10

For God so loved the world, that he gave his one and only Son, that whoever believes in him shall not perish but have everlasting life (JOHN 3:16, NIV).

God loves His creation. He takes pleasure in the marvelous beauties of nature that are the expression of His external wisdom and glory. But God did not give His one and only Son primarily for the great world of nature. It is the world of mankind that called out the highest expression of His love. God loves mankind. He loves them all, rich and poor, wise and simple, friend and enemy, and for them alone He gave His dearest, even His only Son.

Let no one ever feel that no one loves him. Though all human love fails, God's love continues. God's gift of His Son is the unassailable proof of His love for humanity. For this gift, being no less than the gift of God Himself in a way no human mind can fully comprehend, is the eternal demonstration of His love for each one of us.

JUNE 11

Asyncritus (ROMANS 16:14).

Only an ancient name, but it has a very lovely meaning. For Asyncritus signifies "incomparable." Paul knew Asyncritus by name and sent him this greeting. And so the Apostle typifies his Lord. One day, when we see Jesus face to face, He will tell us that we are His Asyncriti—individually incomparable to His great heart. Just as the love of mother and father finds each one of their children incomparable, so Christ in His love treasures each one of us for whom He shed His blood. Yes, we cannot doubt that we are incomparable to our Lord. But dear friend, is He really incomparable to you? Is He more precious and attractive than anything or anyone else?

JUNE 12

For we are unto God a sweet savour of Christ, in them that are saved, and in them that perish: to the one we are the savour of death unto death; and to the other the savour of life unto life (2 CORINTHIANS 2:15, 16a).

For a Christian there is no responsibility more far-reaching than that of witnessing. Eternal issues hang upon the proclamation of the Gospel. And it should sober us believers to realize that this responsibility is one that none of us may evade. We all bear our witness, for we all touch other lives. How many of those lives are we touching as a savor to life? Granted that some may not believe, is it not true that many more would come to Christ were our witness clearer and more powerful? Two people may say exactly the same words about the Lord. In one case the results are nil; in the other there is eternal blessing. Why? One is merely repeating the right words; the other is speaking out of personal faith backed by a consistent life.

Little wonder that Paul cries out in perplexity, "Who is equal to such a calling" (2 Corinthians 2:16, NEB). But there is an answer—the Holy Spirit, who is in us by faith and who is fully equal to the responsibility of being a savor of life or of death to those reached by our witness to our Lord.

JUNE 13

Being made so much better than the angels (HEBREWS 1:4).

"Better." This is a characteristic word of the epistle to the Hebrews, which so highly exalts our Lord. Step by step the comparisons proceed, as the writer exhibits Christ as better than the prophets and the angels, better than Moses and Joshua and Aaron, and as the Mediator of the New Covenant, which is better than the Old.

And how is it with us? Does Christ stand higher in our affections than any other person or thing? Let us search our hearts today in God's presence to find if they contain anything dearer and better to us than Christ. If we do this, we shall find close to our hearts many good things—wife, husband, children, home, friends, work. And they assuredly belong there. But do we also find Christ as our dearest and our best? Nothing else is worthy of the Lord who gave Himself for us.

JUNE 14

And the Lord said unto Gideon, The people that are with thee are too many for me to give the Midianites into their hands, lest Israel vaunt themselves against me, saying, Mine own hand hath saved me (JUDGES 7:2).

What enthusiasm there must have been when thirty-two thousand men from Israel gathered under the banner of Gideon! What consternation must have smitten not only the people but their leader when God drastically cut this army down to ten thousand men (v. 3)! And what folly it must have seemed when these ten thousand were reduced to a band of three hundred (vs. 5, 6)! Three hundred men against the multitudes of Midian; could anything have seemed more foolish than that? The answer is, yes; for these three hundred men were to face their enemy with trumpets, pitchers, and lamps (v. 18). Truly Gideon was a man of valor. It took more moral courage for him to follow God in this strategy than to go out against Midian at the head of a mighty army. But God's ways are not our ways nor his thoughts our thoughts. The one thing necessary for us is to obey God wholly, just as Gideon and his men did, and to do this regardless of the consequences. A chief deterrent to spiritual victory is fear of what might happen should we really go "all out" for our Lord.

JUNE 15

*My days are swifter than a weaver's shuttle, and are spent
without hope* (JOB 7:6).

The first clause is true for every man; the second ought not
be true for any Christian. The older one grows, the swifter time
seems to pass. At the most, we have but a few short years for
service. Moment succeeds moment, hour follows hour, day steps
quickly on the heels of day. Nevertheless, no Christian can
rightly say that his days are spent without hope. Job lived long
before the Gospel age. But where he had nothing beyond in-
timations of redemption, we have the sure hope of being with
our living Redeemer and of being reunited with our dear ones
who are now in His presence. For the New Testament promises
us that we shall be raised in bodies like His glorified body. No
Christian, then, need spend his days without hope. The Bible
gives us the assurance that Jesus is coming. The pledge of His
return is the hope that fortifies our faith and gives us strength
for service.

JUNE 16

*Now this he said about the Spirit, which those who be-
lieved on him were to receive; for as yet the Spirit had
not been given, because Jesus was not yet glorified* (JOHN
7:39, RSV).

The close bond between the Spirit and the glorification of our
Lord is the message of this verse. Where the Spirit is, Christ is
glorified. Where Christ is glorified, there the Spirit is. It
cannot be otherwise. For, as Paul says, "No one can say 'Jesus
is Lord,' except by the Holy Spirit" (1 Corinthians 12:3, RSV).
This being the case, we ought to think about our witness. Is
it aimed first of all at the glorification of Christ? If that is its
aim, then we may trust that the Spirit is in it. The great work
of the Spirit in this age is not to speak of Himself but of Christ.
"When the Spirit of truth comes, he will guide you into all the
truth; for he will not speak on his own authority, but whatever he hears he will speak, and he will declare to you the
things that are to come" (John 16:13, RSV).

JUNE 17

And the streets of the city shall be full of boys and girls playing (ZECHARIAH 8:5).

What a beautiful touch this is in the prophet's description of Israel's blessing in the kingdom age! That time will be one of genuine and glorious restoration. And among its blessings not the least will be children—that deeply satisfying gift of God to man and woman. Here is one of the kingdom joys God even now gives to His own. Let us be thankful for children; while they are a great responsibility, they are also wonderful gifts from our Heavenly Father.

JUNE 18

He . . . laid aside his garments (JOHN 13:4a).

The incident described in this chapter has a symbolic significance. While our Lord laid aside His outer garments in preparation for the lowly service of washing the disciples' feet, in a larger sense this act was typical of what He did when He became incarnate. For there was a time when He put off the garments of His heavenly glory to come down to this earth. Paul tells us that Christ Jesus made Himself of no reputation and took upon Himself the form of a servant (Philippians 2:5-8). Yet it was His eternal state to be in the form of God and equal with God, so that when He entered our world, He gave up transcendent glory no human mind can comprehend.

Now because we have the word of the Lord Jesus Himself that His action in washing the feet of the disciples is an example (v. 15), let us think of the garments we must lay aside in order to follow Him. What are some of them? Well, pride is one. No Christian who wears the cloak of pride can reflect the beautiful humility our Lord exemplified on this occasion. Self-righteousness is another garment to be put away, if we are really to be His disciples. So is indolence. Similar also are the habits and sins that encumber our lives. Are you willing to lay aside anything that is keeping you from serving others in a more Christlike way?

JUNE 19

*My people shall be satisfied with my goodness, saith the
Lord* (JEREMIAH 31:14).

What gives you the greatest satisfaction? Are you highly
pleased with your own goodness, are you contented with your
spiritual attainments? Then you are very far away from the
best God has for you. From Jeremiah's prophecy of the future
restoration of Israel we glean the truth that the ultimate satisfaction is in the Lord's goodness. "My people shall be satisfied
with my goodness." Does not this also imply that in heaven
the redeemed will take their greatest delight in contemplating
the perfect righteousness of Christ rather than considering their
own merits? And if that is to be true in eternity surely now is
the time for us to learn to take our deepest satisfaction in the
wonderful goodness of the Lord.

JUNE 20

*Epaphras . . . a servant of Christ, saluteth you, always
labouring fervently for you in prayers, that ye may stand
perfect and complete in all the will of God* (COLOSSIANS
4:12).

Since Epaphras was in prison with Paul (as may be inferred
from Philemon 23) he could not exercise his gift of preaching.
Yet he remained a servant of Christ and continued his ministry
through prayer. And who would say that he accomplished less
for God during his imprisonment than during his more active
days?

Now among those reading this message today there may be
some modern Epaphrases. Sickrooms can be prisons; circumstances can restrict service. Nevertheless, nothing can limit
prayer. Of all forms of spiritual work it has the widest influence.
From a sickroom it can touch the ends of the earth, from a con-
fined life it can reach up to heaven. But make no mistake;
prayer is spiritual work. Set your mind to pray, and you will
learn how precise Paul's choice of words was, when he described Epaphras as "labouring fervently . . . in prayers."

JUNE 21

Great is thy faithfulness (LAMENTATIONS 3:23b).

Here are four words, perfect in balance and emphasis, that ring with reassurance and strength. They remind us that no Christian should ever question the Lord's faithfulness. We may think of our being partially faithful but never of His being anything but completely so. The Lord is absolutely trustworthy in everything. His is the only perfect integrity. Therefore, we may rest our lives wholly upon Him. Whatever happens to us, the Lord remains faithful in all His ways. Though we prove faithless, He always keeps His promises. Nothing, not even the tragedies of life, can alter His unchanging reliability. When we learn to see, as did Jeremiah in this elegy on the fall of Jerusalem, not only the Lord's faithfulness but also the sheer greatness of that faithfulness, we shall have more of His peace in our hearts. No wonder Jeremiah went on in the next verse to declare: "The Lord is my portion, saith my soul; therefore will I hope in him."

JUNE 22

With joy you will draw water from the wells of salvation (ISAIAH 12:3, RSV).

A happy promise for every Christian to claim! For what is Christian service, if not drawing water out of the wells of salvation? These wells are inexhaustible. In them there is water enough to quench the thirst of all the world. And our high privilege as servants of Christ is to give the thirsty people water to drink. All this is true and inspiring. But there is even more in the promise. There is, for one thing, the little phrase, "with joy."

Think of a servant of Jesus Christ dispensing the living water and doing it with a gloomy countenance and melancholy spirit? Yet that sometimes happens. Thank God, the water is the water of life. Whether we who draw it are happy or not, it remains the water of life. We miss much when we fail to see that the Lord wants us to serve and witness "with joy." Our God is God of light, and He calls us to happy service for Him.

JUNE 23

Your enemy the devil prowls around like a roaring lion looking for someone to devour. Resist him, standing firm in the faith (1 PETER 5:8, 9, NIV).

Peter's description of the devil as a roaring lion looking for someone to swallow up (the literal meaning of the verb "devour") is by no means overdrawn. Our enemy is very terrible and his strength far outmatches our own, which makes the Apostle's advice all the more surprising. Although the traveler would naturally flee from the lion, the Christian is to resist the devil. But there is something that makes all the difference between victory and defeat. It is the place where we resist. "Resist him," writes Peter, "standing firm in the faith." Everything depends upon where you stand when the devil attacks you. "Standing firm in the faith" is another way of saying "abiding in Christ." Believers who stand their ground, abiding in Christ, are safe from the enemy, even though he "prowls around like a roaring lion."

JUNE 24

And Moses did look upon all the work, and, behold, they had done it as the Lord had commanded, even so had they done it: and Moses blessed them (EXODUS 48:43).

What a happy day it was when the tabernacle was completed! The work had been liberally provided for, faithfully executed, and joyfully consummated. Now the great leader of Israel inspected it. All the revealed details of its construction had been carried out. Then came the reward. "And Moses blessed them." Observe that it was not the tabernacle Moses blessed, but the workmen.

We Christians are like Bezalel and his helpers. We are building a temple which is the Church of the living God. Each of us is a living stone in that eternal structure, as Peter says in his first epistle (1 Peter 2:5). We are not responsible for the whole structure, but only for those parts that are ourselves. One day the work will be done. Then it will not be a Moses who looks upon our work, but the Lord Jesus Himself. Happy the Christians in that day who, having built their lives as the Lord has commanded, receive His own blessing!

JUNE 25

So I ate it, and it tasted as sweet as honey (EZEKIEL 3:3, NEB).

After receiving a message regarding the rebellion of Israel, Ezekiel looked and saw a hand with a scroll. The scroll, written on both sides, contained "lamentations and mourning and woe" (2:9, 10). Then God told Ezekiel to eat it. The scroll stands for God's message to the prophet. Bitter and tragic though that message was, still to Ezekiel it was also sweet.

This paradox relates to God's servants at all times. Every mature Christian can remember occasions when God's will has seemed very difficult. Sometimes we shrink from it, because we fear what it will do to us. But when we go all the way and do what God asks us, we find a strange and wonderful sweetness even in our hard experiences. God may invite us to do difficult things for Him, yet when we do them we may trust Him to give us His peace that passes understanding.

JUNE 26

And I fell at his feet to worship him. And he said unto me, See thou do it not: I am thy fellow servant, and of thy brethren that have the testimony of Jesus: worship God: for the testimony of Jesus is the spirit of prophecy (REVELATION 19:10).

John had been hearing the voice of one of God's angelic messengers. So overwhelming were the things told him that in his vision the Apostle fell at the feet of the messenger to worship him. Then followed one of the most important statements in Revelation. Repudiating worship of himself by saying that he was only a fellow servant with John, the messenger said: "Worship God: for the testimony of Jesus is the spirit of prophecy."

Right here is the most essential of all principles for interpreting the prophetic Word. What is prophecy? It is "the testimony of Jesus." Its main purpose is to point, in type and figure, directly or indirectly, to the Saviour. Therefore, to depart from this principle by laying emphasis in prophetic study elsewhere than on the main current of Messianic truth is to risk falling into dangerous vagaries of interpretation. Christ is at the heart of prophecy as well as of all other portions of the Word of God

JUNE 27

I have compassion on the multitude, because they have now been with me three days, and have nothing to eat (MARK 8:2).

In this verse and the companion passage in Matthew 15:32, the Lord Jesus used a verb that reveals the tenderness of His heart. The Authorized Version translates it, "I have compassion," but in doing so misses something of its meaning. The verb is related to the Greek term for the innermost heart or seat of the emotions. It therefore means being concerned to the bottom of one's heart. Weymouth well translated it: "my heart aches."

But if the Lord Jesus used this tender word, if His heart ached, let us ask, "Why?" Well, our Lord's heart ached because of the need of the multitude that had followed Him. The thing that always stirs His heart is human need. Long before the foundation of the world, the Eternal Son foresaw the need of man; out of the depth of His everlasting love He was willing to humble Himself and become obedient to death for our sake. Calvary is the ultimate expression of the Saviour's heart, moved with pity for lost humanity. How then can we ever remain unmoved by the human misery we see around us in the world today?

JUNE 28

Honour the Lord with thy substance (PROVERBS 3:9a).

Look well at these words, and then ask yourself, "Have I been doing it?" "Oh, yes," you reply. "I have my church envelope. I set aside a portion of my means for the Lord." That is good, but there is more to the command than that. "Honour the Lord," it says, "with thy substance." Not "with one tenth, or one quarter, or one-half of thy substance," but simply and inclusively "with thy substance." "What," you ask, "give everything away?" Yes and no. Yes, in that everything a Christian has must be used to honor God. No, in that God expects us to retain some things for our own needs. But whether our substance is given away or used personally, the principle remains that with it all we are to honor the Lord. How the waste of Christian money would be cut down if we would just ask, "Am I honoring the Lord with my substance?"

JUNE 29

I charge you to keep the commandment stainless and irreproachable until the appearance of our Lord Jesus Christ (1 TIMOTHY 6:14, Berkeley).

To what commandment is Paul referring? Read back a few sentences and you will see that it relates to Christian behavior and culminates in these words: "Fight the good fight of faith, lay hold on eternal life" (v. 12). This stirring command applies to Christians in these times just as much as it did to young Timothy, to whom Paul originally addressed it. For we are all engaged in the universal warfare against evil. Whatever else it may be, the Christian life is a conflict.

The old saying that all's fair in love and war can never apply to our combat. We must indeed "fight the good fight," but, as the Apostle says in our text for today, we are to do so keeping the commandment "stainless and irreproachable." Nothing of evil, nothing of compromise, nothing short of full integrity may be done by us. We have to wield the sword of the Spirit with all our might, but we have to wield it honestly and cleanly.

JUNE 30

I blessed the most High, and I praised and honoured him that liveth forever . . . (DANIEL 4:34b).

These words and those that follow them (verses 34, 35) comprise one of the most remarkable portions of Scripture—a psalm of praise spoken by a pagan king. Pagan though he was, Nebuchadnezzar had chance after chance through the ministry of Daniel to recognize the supremacy of God. And he did compliment God with his lips, though his heart remained fixed in its pride, so that he ascribed the greatness of Babylon solely to himself. But God will be praised. He must be glorified. So after years of disciplinary judgment, Nebuchadnezzar voiced this remarkable hymn of praise to God.

If these things apply to a pagan, how much more do they relate to us Christians! Yes, we owe God the constant praise of our hearts. Ingratitude is base, and it is a positive sin for a Christian to let even a day go by without praise to God. If there is one element in our prayer and worship that is essential, surely it is praise.

JULY 1

And when they had prayed, the place was shaken where they were assembled together; and they were all filled with the Holy Ghost, and they spake the word of God with boldness (Acts 4:31).

"When they had prayed." There is the key to the shaking of the place and the infilling with the Spirit and the speaking with boldness. The connection is causal, not just one of time sequence. Because they first prayed, power came. There is, then, an essential preliminary for Christian service no matter what it may be. And that is prayer first. Let us make it our practice not to live a single day, not to give a single testimony, never to do anything for our Lord apart from prayer.

JULY 2

Thus saith the Lord; Stand in the court of the Lord's house, and speak . . . all the words that I command thee (JEREMIAH 26:2).

"Now it came to pass, when Jeremiah had made an end of speaking all that the Lord had commanded him . . . all the people took him, saying, Thou shalt surely die" (v. 8). What a response to the Lord's messenger! See how the opposition to the prophet had been mounting. He had just obeyed God in standing "in the court of the Lord's house," where he had continued his message of judgment. But the reward he received from the people with whom he was pleading was "Thou shalt surely die." What did the prophet have to say to that threat? "As for me," he replied, "behold, I am in your hand: do with me as seemeth good and meet unto you" (v. 14).

Jeremiah is not an easy book to read, but once we begin to penetrate beneath the surface, we can hardly fail to be stirred by the moral greatness of the prophet. Faced in this case with death, he showed brave resignation. With calm assurance, he placed himself in the hands of the Lord. And he won out. "Then said the princes and all the people unto the priests and to the prophets; This man is not worthy to die: for he hath spoken to us in the name of the Lord our God" (v. 16). For the time being the call to repent and turn back to the Lord continued to resound in the doomed city. Once more faith triumphed, as it so often does when exercised with courage and integrity.

JULY 3

The elder unto the elect lady and her children, whom I love in the truth (2 JOHN 1a).

Here is the basis of all Christian fellowship—love "in the truth." Neither personal attractiveness, nor wealth, fame, or human character constitute the tie that binds our hearts together. Only our love for the truth does this. And the truth is a Person, not a philosophical abstraction. The Lord Jesus Christ is *the* Truth. In Him all Christians may be united in fellowship. Cultivate your friends in the Lord. Pray with them, talk with them about spiritual things and about the daily business of living. Christian fellowship is one of the greatest joys we have.

JULY 4

The pride of your heart has deceived you (OBADIAH 3, RSV).

On this day of national observance let us think about this word of God, which came long ago to the nation of Edom. History shows that the doom pronounced against that people by Jeremiah, Obadiah, Ezekiel, and others of the prophets has been fulfilled. And God's righteous dealings with Edom clearly stand as a warning for all nations in all ages.

Here, then, was a nation that thought it could get along without God. Self-sufficient in the isolation of its mountain stronghold, it lived only to itself and in its proud heart harbored a perpetual hatred against its kinsfolk, Israel. But God dealt with it in summary judgment.

Oh, the tragedy of the "Edomites" today! Whole governments, like the U.S.S.R. and Communist China, thinking that they can banish God! Other nations, like our own country, going the way of Edom through indifference and sheer default; plans being made and policies determined with the Almighty left out of the reckoning. Such is the way of Edom. Let us Christians pray for our country that it may yet turn from self-sufficiency to the living God. And let us be careful to take God into account in everything we do, lest we also slip into the sin of Edom.

JULY 5

We wrestle not against flesh and blood (EPHESIANS 6:12a).

In telling Christians how to wage the spiritual warfare, Paul employs a distinctly physical term. "We wrestle," he says, using the actual Greek word for the fiercest kind of hand to hand, body to body, struggle. There's nothing impersonal about this spiritual wrestling. It means grappling with the foe and having it out, till one or the other of the combatants sinks down exhausted. You and I can do some things in this life by proxy. We can shift responsibilities and find substitutes. But we can never wrestle for God by proxy. No one can take our place in the personal encounter with the adversary of God and of our souls.

JULY 6

Then the same day at evening, being the first day of the week, when the doors were shut where the disciples were assembled for fear of the Jews, came Jesus and stood in the midst, and saith unto them, Peace be unto you (JOHN 20:19).

In the Gospel accounts of the post-Resurrection appearances of the Lord Jesus, one message from His lips is several times repeated. It is this, "Peace be unto you." Let us think back to that evening long ago. There was the little company of disciples huddled together in a locked room. Nevertheless Jesus came and stood in the midst. For His presence is always with His own, no matter where they are, so long as they are looking to Him. Wherever His disciples are in need, there He is.

"Peace be unto you." In that word of benediction is centered the whole of our Lord's work. His ministry, culminating in the cross and the empty tomb, is a reconciling ministry. He came and died and rose again that we, who are by nature the enemies of God, might be brought back to the Father. Christ has made the only peace that endures forever. He alone is able to confer on troubled souls the peace that passes understanding. How personal His message is! "Peace," He says, "be unto *you*." Christ's peace is a personal gift, a matter between our Lord and us.

JULY 7

And in thy seed shall all the nations of the earth be blessed, because thou hast obeyed my voice (GENESIS 22:18).

Consider God's reason for blessing all nations of the earth through Abraham. "Because," said God, "thou hast obeyed my voice." That is why Abraham became the channel of universal blessing. How very much depends on obedience! Think of Abraham. Upon the obedience of this one man depended worldwide spiritual blessing.

Obedience is one of the most fateful things in life. We may think it a simple thing to disobey God. But the ramifications of a single act of disobedience may be very extensive. Scientists who deal with atomic power speak of chain reactions. One thing sets off another till overwhelming force results. But the spiritual realm also has its chain reactions. Either obedience or disobedience to God may be the source of results so incommensurable and far-reaching as to stagger the imagination. To obey God consistently and faithfully in the daily round of life is never a small thing.

JULY 8

And King Rehoboam made in their stead shields of bronze, and committed them to the hands of the officers of the guard, who kept the door of the king's house (1 KINGS 14:27, RSV).

When Shishak, king of Egypt, despoiled the royal palace at Jerusalem of Solomon's golden shields, Rehoboam replaced them with shields of bronze. The populace may have been deceived by the subterfuge. But God knew the pretense for what it was, and caused it to be written down in Scripture for all the world to see.

Rehoboam's expedience is still being practised. Outward religious acts may be displayed as shields of bronze, yet all the time the gold of true faith is lacking. But God knows. Woe to that man who is depending for salvation upon his own life and attainments. Bright as they may look, in the sight of a holy God they are but tarnished bronze. All, even the best of us, have our bronze shields. Only the righteousness of Christ, imputed to us through faith, can withstand the searching gaze of the Almighty.

JULY 9

If any man's will is to do his will, he shall know whether the teaching is from God or whether I am speaking on my own authority (JOHN 7:17, RSV).

This is one of the great declarations of our Lord. It shows how anyone may know the reality of His teaching. To those who say they want to believe but can't, to the Christian who hesitates to launch out in full dependence on the promises of Christ, it offers an experiment. Reduced to its simplest terms that experiment amounts to this: Submit your will to God and you will know. Just as surely as it is impossible for God to lie, so everyone who honestly says to God, "I will do Thy will," will know whether the Lord Jesus spoke divine truth or only a human word. In light of this, it is the unsurrendered will that keeps men from knowing the Lord Jesus Christ. No man can hold full title to his own will and at the same time really know God. Nor can a Christian hold partial title to his own will and realize to the full what the Lord can do in his life.

JULY 10

Favour is deceitful, and beauty is vain: but a woman that feareth the Lord, she shall be praised (PROVERBS 31:30).

The imagery of this passage (vv. 10-31) is old-fashioned, but the virtues it describes are timeless. Here is the classic portrait of godly womanhood. Here is the kind of mother who nurtured an Augustine, a Lincoln, or a Wesley. And there are still such women! Customs differ and externals change; no longer is the wife and mother responsible for weaving clothes and planting vineyards. Yet the criteria of Christian womanhood remain the same.

Now it is significant that this portrait presents no shade of weakness. On the contrary, several times the ideal wife is linked to strength (vv. 17, 25). Why, the schedule implied for her day could only have been carried out by a woman of stamina! And at the end of this word picture, we find the foundation of it all. "Favour is deceitful, and beauty is vain: but a woman that feareth the Lord, she shall be praised." In respect to essential spiritual virtues, there is no difference between man and woman. The fear of the Lord is the basis for virtuous womanhood no less than for godly manhood.

JULY 11

*How often I have longed to gather your children together
... but you were not willing* (MATTHEW 23:37, NIV).

Looking out over the city so soon to betray Him, the Lord
Jesus voiced His will to gather His erring people to His loving
heart. But knowing everything, even the heart of man, He had
to conclude with that realistic acknowledgement of human rebellion, "but you were not willing."

In the Greek Testament this passage contains in each instance the strong word for will or desire, *thelo*. So it sets
before us the spiritual conflict of the ages—Christ's supreme desire for man to come to Him versus man's stubborn desire to
resist Christ's saving invitation. Oh, the sadness of those words,
"but you were not willing." In them is tragedy. Because men
will not come to Christ, sin continues and sorrows increase.

What about us? Does our Lord ever have to say of us, as He
looks into our hearts and sees our obstinate refusal of His will,
"but you were not willing"?

JULY 12

*And he said, O Lord God of my master Abraham, I pray
thee, send me good speed this day, and shew kindness unto
my master Abraham* (GENESIS 24:12).

Abraham had given explicit instructions to his servant as
to how he was to seek a bride for Isaac. But there was one thing
that servant did which his master Abraham did not command
him to do. As soon as he came to Nahor, he paused for prayer.
"O Lord God of my master Abraham," he said, "I pray thee,
send me good speed this day, and shew kindness unto my master
Abraham." What a perfect prayer for a servant! He asked nothing for himself; all his concern was for his master. This servant
exercised his spiritual initiative in doing the one additional thing
that would help him to be fully obedient.

The vast majority of us Christians, so far as outward acclaim
goes, are among the Lord's unknown servants. Others may have
little knowledge of what we do, but each of us has a task to do
for our Master. Would that we might accomplish it in the
prayerful spirit of this servant of long ago!

JULY 13

And after the fire a still small voice (1 KINGS 19:12).

Read it again—that marvelous description of Elijah on Horeb (1 Kings 19:8-18). And as you read it, picture the lonely prophet on the mountain. See the tornado, the earthquake, and the fire, and learn that the Lord was in none of these. Then hear the still small voice.

Do you know how to listen to God? It takes quietness of soul to hear Him, the quietness that comes only to the trusting heart. He will speak to us, inwardly and gently, as we have communion with Him in prayer and in reading His Word. May we be receptive to His voice today.

JULY 14

When Jehu came to Jezreel, Jezebel heard of it; and she painted her eyes, and adorned her head, and looked out of the window (2 KINGS 9:30, RSV).

Here is Jezebel's portrait, done from life, just a few moments before her shameful end. She knew who Jehu was. She understood that the avenger had at last come. Yet sin never reforms. We read the words and almost see the painted, brazen face staring impudently out of the palace window.

What could be done for Jezebel at that time in her life? The answer may well be "nothing." She had gone too far in deliberate iniquity to be salvaged. But Jezebel was not always thus. There was a time when it might have been different. Like all men and women she had stood at the crossroads between good and evil, heaven and hell. She chose the downward path and, whenever an opportunity came for her to go the other way, she kept her feet on the road to ruin. So retribution, even to the literal fulfillment of the prophesied doom (vv. 36, 37), caught up with her.

The story of Jezebel has something to say to our times. She is not merely a character of ancient Israel; she lives again in the pages of modern fiction, is embodied on the screen, and her depravity is applauded by multitudes. How long can people retain their virtue, while filling their minds with books and pictures that scorn the most elementary Christian morality? Read Romans 1:32 in context and think about it as God's comment on the debasement of culture today.

JULY 15

Is it well with the child? And she answered, It is well (2 KINGS 4:26b).

What faith the Shunamite showed! Her boy was lying dead at home, but she met the servant of Elisha and said, "It is well." What had she done? She had placed her burden, in this case her dead son, on the bed of the man of God—that is, before God—and then she had shut the door on him. She believed that God through Elisha would raise her son up. And God did. What a picture of how you and I may leave our own burdens with the Lord!

JULY 16

I saw in the night visions, and behold, one like the Son of man came with the clouds of heaven, and came to the Ancient of days, and they brought him near before him. And there was given him dominion, and glory, and a kingdom, that all people, nations, and languages, should serve him; his dominion is an everlasting dominion, which shall not pass away, and his kingdom that which shall not be destroyed (DANIEL 7:13, 14).

So long as men interpret Scripture differently, there will be wide divergence of opinion regarding the meaning of the prophecies of Daniel. But regardless of differences, these passages contain certain central affirmations of prophecy on which Christians may agree. And surely this is one of these affirmations. How we need its glorious optimism! Ours too is a time for night visions. But those who really believe the prophetic Word can discern the promise of victory in and through the Son of man, who is surely coming "with the clouds of heaven." One day the imperial investiture Daniel describes will take place. One day Christ will be given His heritage of "dominion, and glory, and a kingdom, that all people, nations, and languages should serve him." The optimism of Bible prophecy is no mere dream; it is an assured hope, based upon the eternal person and everlasting kingdom of the Son of man, our Saviour Jesus Christ.

JULY 17

Now we know that all things are working together for good to those who love God, who are called according to the Divine purpose (ROMANS 8:28, Weymouth).

Sometimes just a turn of phrase brings out a shade of meaning in a well-loved promise. Take for example the verb in this rendering of Romans 8:28. "All things are working together for good to those who love God. . . ." It is not just the future to which the promise applies, but the present. God's beneficent supervision of our lives is a continual thing. While we may indeed trust Him to bend every occasion in our lives to His perfect will, it is our present right to count upon His doing that very thing here and now. The process of God's sovereign superintendence over our lives began the moment we entered into His family by faith, and it has been continuing ever since. Oh, Christian friend, let us believe that today, at this very moment when we are reading these words, God is actively at work in our behalf, making everything—yes, the events of this day and even this present hour—work together to accomplish His purpose for good in our lives!

JULY 18

They shall perish; but thou remainest; and they all shall wax old as doth a garment (HEBREWS 1:11).

It is the earth and the heavens, the very physical universe about us, that is here spoken of as aging and perishing. In contrast, we are reminded that the Lord remains unchangeable: "But thou art the same, and thy years shall not fail" (v. 12). The author of Hebrews is making an impressive contrast between the changing world and the unchanging Christ. Nothing in the universe is static. One looks, for example, at the great mountains. How secure and remote they seem, majestic and aloof in their snow-clad splendor. Then one looks closer, and sees that the mountains are changing. The glaciers are moving, the rocks crumbling; daily the mountains are succumbing to the destiny of all material things. But Christ is different. He is different because He is eternal, without beginning and without end. He never changes. Therefore, true security is found only in the soul's union with Him who remains and whose years shall not fail.

JULY 19

Beginning at Moses and all the prophets, he expounded unto them in all the scriptures the things concerning himself (Luke 24:27).

What a Bible lesson those two discouraged believers had as they walked toward Emmaus! To them the written Word was opened by Him who is the living Word. No wonder that later, after the risen Lord had vanished from their sight, they said, "Did not our hearts burn within us, while he talked with us by the way, and while he opened to us the scriptures?" (v. 32).

Now our Lord did a very wonderful thing for those humble disciples; He not only personally opened to them the Scriptures, but He also gave them the key with which they themselves might unlock the Book after His departure: "He expounded unto them in all the scriptures the things concerning himself." Christ Himself is the key to the Scriptures. There is no simpler and more rewarding method of Bible study than to seek Him in the Book. Search the Word for Him. There is no portion of Scripture that will not open to this key, prayerfully and faithfully applied.

JULY 20

And they told what things were done in the way, and how he was known of them in the breaking of bread (Luke 24:35).

"In the breaking of bread." Though sometimes used of the communion, the phrase in this place takes a wider meaning from its context. As verse 30 shows, it refers to the evening meal in which the Lord Jesus joined at Emmaus and during which He was made known. Bearing this in mind helps us understand the abiding lesson of our verse for today. The same Christ who was made known to His disciples in that humble village meal long ago is still present in the simple things of life. The breaking of bread may still be an occasion for His manifestation. The family table, dedicated to Him through prayer, bears witness not only to mutual love but also discloses to our guests the very presence of the unseen Guest. There are few more winsome testimonies than the Christian home where the Lord is honored while the daily bread is broken.

JULY 21

And so were the churches established in the faith, and increased in number daily (ACTS 16:5).

Here is one of the principles for building up a church. Let a church's people be established (the word in the original means "strengthened") in the faith, and it will grow. This principle worked in the first century, and it will work today. If certain churches have lost power, it is not because the Christian faith is any less efficacious than in apostolic times, but simply because those churches are suffering from spiritual malnutrition. When a congregation is fed the Word of God by a believing and dedicated minister, it receives the spiritual sustenance that makes enduring growth possible.

There are plenty of other methods for building up churches. Some of them are very useful; but all of them must, to be truly effective, rest upon establishing the people of God in the faith.

JULY 22

The Judge is standing at the door! (JAMES 5:9b, NIV).

"The Judge is standing at the door!" What a vivid way of stating the inevitability of meeting Christ. However we interpret the thought of the door, the fact of it remains. If we say that the door is death and thus, as some do, lay aside the thought of the Lord's coming in person, we do not escape the Judge. For when we go out of this life through death, there He is, standing before that door. Or if we visualize the Judge standing before the door of heaven, ready in His time, which for us may be any time, to come again, we are still confronted with the fact of meeting Him. Oh, that all of us might realize that the Judge who stands before the door cannot be evaded! "The Lord's coming is near" (v. 8, NIV). One day He will come through the door, and then we shall stand before Him. Are we ready to meet Him?

JULY 23

And he said unto Moses, Come up unto the Lord, thou, and Aaron, Nadab, and Abihu, and seventy of the elders of Israel; and worship ye afar off (Exodus 24:1).

"Worship ye afar off." That is characteristic of the Old Testament approach to God. It was necessarily through priests, sacrifices, and offerings. Even Aaron in this instance was to keep his distance; only Moses could come near the Lord (v. 2). To be sure, this particular stipulation was for the interval between the giving of the law and the completion of the tabernacle. Nevertheless it is an example of the Old Testament order that, after the tabernacle was set up and later when the temple was built, stressed the barrier between man and God.

How different it all became when the Lord Jesus died for our sins! Even we Gentiles, "who sometimes were far off," are "now in Christ Jesus . . . made nigh by the blood of Christ" (Ephesians 2:13). We have no greater Christian privilege than that of access to God through His dear Son. Then why are we so slow in using that privilege in the daily practice of prayer?

JULY 24

For Ezra had prepared his heart to seek the law of the Lord, and to do it, and to teach in Israel statutes and judgments (Ezra 7:10).

In Proverbs we read, "Keep thy heart with all diligence; for out of it are the issues of life" (Proverbs 4:23). This principle is illustrated by Ezra. He was blessed in the leadership of his people because he had first of all fitted his heart for service. Before endeavoring to teach Israel the law of the Lord, Ezra had brought his own inner life into conformity with it and practiced it in his actions. So with us. The best preparation for preaching is the heart preparation of the preacher. The best way for a Christian to fit himself for witnessing is to make sure that the things he testifies about are real to his own heart. None of us has any right to insist on teaching others truths to which we ourselves are not committed. Let us be sure that we are not trying to lead others to higher spiritual ground than we ourselves are willing to stand on.

JULY 25

We have an advocate with the Father (1 JOHN 2:1b).

Consider the present tense of this declaration. We have—
right now—an advocate with the Father. Tomorrow He will still
be our advocate. He is always our advocate. Think of an advocate as a lawyer, and you catch something of the thought. Business enterprises engage a counsel; he is the advocate of the firm,
always ready to represent it at the bar of justice whenever
occasion arises. So with our advocate, Jesus Christ the righteous;
He is our divine counsel before the Father. Always, in every
case, without exception, He is in the presence of God to plead
for His redeemed. And what a plea He makes as He presents
His precious blood as the atoning sacrifice for our sin!

JULY 26

In the beginning God created the heaven and the earth
(GENESIS 1:1).

No more important single statement has ever been made than
this opening verse of the Word of God. Here in ten words we
have the one sure foundation of everything.

This sentence contains the answer to all false views of the
origin of things. Materialism, which claims that matter is
eternal, is answered, because we are told that God created the
heaven and the earth. Pantheism, which confuses God and
the universe, is likewise silenced, because the Creator is distinct
from what He has created. So also polytheism with its many
gods is doomed by the mention of the one true God. And as for
atheism, which denies God utterly, it too is banished by the
very naming of the Deity; while agnosticism, which claims
that nothing can be known about God, is refuted by this au-
thoritative word as to His creative power. Truly this majestic
declaration is the sure foundation on which everything rests.

JULY 27

Beloved, think it not strange concerning the fiery trial which is to try you, as though some strange thing happened unto you (1 PETER 4:12).

"Beloved, think it not strange . . . ." But that is just what we who are beloved of God *do* think. Fiery trial tests us, and we sigh and cry out, "Oh, what a strange providence this is! How unusual a temptation has come to me!" when all the time we should be looking to God and saying, "Yes, Lord, I understand. These things are not strange; they are to be expected. I recognize that 'all that will live godly in Christ Jesus shall suffer persecution'" (2 Timothy 3:12). So let us not complicate the fiery trials that inevitably come to us by bemoaning their strangeness. Simply accepting them as part of our pilgrimage will help us to bear them as we look to God for strength.

JULY 28

He shall glorify me, for he shall receive of mine, and shall shew it unto you (JOHN 16:14).

According to this statement of our Lord, the office of the Spirit in our time is not to point to Himself but to glorify Christ. This is emphatically expressed in the Greek text of the words on which we are meditating today. "That One" (the demonstrative pronoun is used), said the Lord Jesus, "shall glorify me." And the word "me" is the emphatic form of the personal pronoun.

Christians are less well instructed regarding the Holy Spirit than any other major doctrine. Many are strangely ignorant of His relationship to them and the marvelous work to which God has appointed Him. On the other hand, there are those who, going to the other extreme, fall into a kind of preoccupation with the Holy Spirit. This great passage, however, presents the true place of the Spirit. It defines His office in this age and makes very plain His Christ-exalting work. We may take it as a rule of the Christian life that the more we are filled with the Spirit the more we shall glorify the Lord Jesus.

JULY 29

A little while, and ye shall not see me, and again, a little while, and ye shall see me ... (JOHN 16:16).

There is great comfort in these words, "a little while." They assure us, just as they assured the disciples of the first century, that we shall soon see our Lord. "A little while"—yes, it can only be "a little while"! Have you ever thought that there are but two possibilities in respect to us Christians seeing the Lord Jesus? Either He delays His return till after our death, or He comes before we die. At the most, just the completion of our span of life separates us from the presence of our Lord. At the least, it may be today when He comes. Think of it, Christian friend! We are absolutely certain to see the Lord Jesus soon. In just "a little while," as He has said, we will be like Him when we see Him as He is (1 John 3:2). What, then, does this say to us about how we are living?

JULY 30

Who hath measured the waters in the hollow of his hand, and meted out heaven with the span, and comprehended the dust of the earth in a measure, and weighed the mountains in scales, and the hills in a balance? (ISAIAH 40:12).

Here is a question, surely one of the most sublime ever asked. But it is a mistake to regard it only as rhetorical, introduced by the prophet merely for literary effect. On the contrary, it embodies an inquiry everyone must answer.

"Who is it," God is asking us, "who has made everything and who controls all things?" Well, some would reply that it is merely an impersonal force that has done all this; others would relegate these vast activities to a materialistic process like evolution. But the Christian knows that only the heavenly Father is great enough to cup the oceans in His hand, to survey the heavens with His outstretched arm, and to balance the mountains in His scales. We believers can never overestimate the greatness of our God. And according to His greatness, so is His ability to deal in perfect wisdom with those who trust in Him.

JULY 31

He that dwelleth in the secret place of the most High shall abide under the shadow of the Almighty (PSALM 91:1).

From this great psalm have flowed unceasing streams of blessing. As we look at this opening verse, we note that it is in the nature of an address, pointing out the kind of person for whom the psalm is meant. For its comforting phrases are not for everybody. One cannot live a secular and God-forgetting life, and then expect without any change of heart to share these blessings. The Ninety-first Psalm is addressed to a definite kind of person, described in this initial sentence as "he that dwelleth in the secret place of the most High."

Now when we find Scripture speaking by way of particular designation, we should be careful to seek an exact interpretation. Let us note, therefore, that the psalm is for him "that dwelleth in the secret place of the most High"; the occasional sojourner in "the secret place" cannot fully claim its assurance. It is for those who dwell—that is to say, for those who are living in God's presence all the time.

What is "the secret place of the most High"? For the psalmist it may have been the tabernacle or temple. For us Christians it certainly signifies our access to God through our Lord Jesus Christ (Romans 5:1, 2). It is not enough for us to spend an hour or two a week in the secret place. We must be living before the Lord, yes, *in* the Lord, so constantly that we may be said to dwell in Him. Only thus are we fully under "the shadow of the Almighty," who is our refuge and fortress, our God in whom we trust.

AUGUST 1

Thou walkest in the truth (3 JOHN 3b).

In the first part of this little letter John holds up his friend Gaius as an example of authentic Christian living. What a compliment he pays him in these words: "Thou walkest in the truth." Gaius's life spoke for Christ; he walked the Gospel. How generous God is! We may have failed yesterday to walk the Gospel. But with each dawn we have a new chance to walk the truth. Let us, however, bear in mind that either through the Lord's return or through our being called home in death there will come a last day, a last chance for us to walk our faith. How important, then, to serve God faithfully today.

AUGUST 2

And that night they caught nothing (JOHN 21:3b).

Superficially we may say that Peter and the others returned to their fishing in self-will. Therefore, they worked all night without success. But this presupposes that they did wrong in turning at this time to their nets, and this is by no means certain. It was the time between Christ's resurrection and His ascension. The disciples' means were slender, and, as they were waiting during this mysterious period, they might well have run out of food. So they really needed to return, if only briefly, to their work as fishermen.

Why, then, were they so unsuccessful? May not a reason be that our Lord was preparing them for the blessing He was so soon to pour out on them? He knew that before they received that blessing they must in their own hearts learn some lessons. Galilee teems with fish. But Christ is Lord of all; His power certainly extends to "the fish of the sea, and whatsoever passeth through the paths of the seas" (Psalm 8:8). His restraining hand may well have kept them from catching fish that night. For He Himself was standing on the shore (v. 4) to teach the disciples new lessons of service.

Have we come to some barren places in our lives? Are we facing discouragement and lack of success? Then is the time for us to take heart, realizing that the Lord Jesus may be letting us experience these things for His own good purpose in fitting us for His service

AUGUST 3

Behold, I have refined thee, but not with silver; I have chosen thee in the furnace of affliction (ISAIAH 48:10).

Though we are base metal, God sees more in us than we can ever imagine. He is the true alchemist, able to do what none other in the universe can ever do. He can take the iron and clay of our lives. He can put them into "the furnace of affliction"; and lo! out of the flames comes the gold of unwavering faith and high service. Every Christian is an example of transmutation in the spiritual realm. His redemption is a miracle of change. But the God who redeemed us at the cost of giving His own Son to go through the furnace of affliction is at work upon us all our days. In daily life He teaches us what the furnace of affliction means. Let us not be afraid of it. It is a blessed place, because out of it God takes some of His choicest servants. Honored is the Christian who has been chosen in the furnace of affliction.

AUGUST 4

I thank God, whom I serve from my forefathers with pure conscience, that without ceasing I have remembrance of thee in my prayers night and day (2 TIMOTHY 1:3).

These words must have been of great encouragement to Timothy, separated as he was from the veteran Apostle. Paul was soon to undergo martyrdom. But like his Lord, he sought not self-comfort but the welfare of his loved ones. We may be certain that all his life Timothy treasured this assurance of Paul's unceasing prayers.

How eloquently this verse speaks of the Apostle's own prayer life. Think of being able to write that you are praying for someone without ceasing night and day! The sheer persistence of Paul's prayer life inspires us who have so much to learn about what it means to be continually before the throne of grace. Paul was a spiritual giant. And one of the reasons for his greatness was that he actually *lived* in the attitude of prayer. Night and day, his heart was constantly before the Lord interceding for others.

AUGUST 5

Ye must be born again (JOHN 3:7b).

One of the great spiritual needs today is a more adequate grasp of what regeneration is. To be born again actually means what it says. Regeneration is a new birth and nothing less. Reformation is no substitute; nor is transformation a satisfactory equivalent. As Paul said, "If any man be in Christ, he is a new creature; old things are passed away; behold, all things are become new" (2 Corinthians 5:17).

The old nature cannot be reformed; it is sinful and incorrigible. The old self-life can never rise higher than itself. Only the new life in Christ can see God.

It's all very well for us to claim that we are born again. But do we have the new heart Christ alone can give? Are we really new creatures, "created in Christ Jesus for good works, which God prepared beforehand, that we should walk in them" (Ephesians 2:10, RSV)?

AUGUST 6

Remember the sabbath day, to keep it holy (EXODUS 20:8).

One of the errors of our time is the widespread disregard of the Lord's Day. To consider the keeping of that day a mere religious custom developed by the ancient Hebrews is a serious mistake. The principle of a day of rest is not just a matter of custom; it is grounded in creation and has its basis in the example of God Himself. No rational person with the least bit of reverence for the Almighty would deny that He knew what He was doing when He made all things. "And on the seventh day God ended his work which he had made; and he rested on the seventh day from all his work which he had made" (Genesis 2:2). Whether we like it or not, we are so made as to require a day of cessation from the daily routine. Moreover, for our souls' health we must take time to worship our Maker. The Resurrection led the Church to set aside the first day for this purpose, yet the principle remains unchanged. It is not a question merely of details of the observance of the Lord's Day. We are so made as to require the Sabbath rest, and we impoverish body and soul by neglecting it.

AUGUST 7

And he brought me to the door of the court; and when I looked, behold a hole in the wall (EZEKIEL 8:7).

Reading on from this curious statement, we see a remarkable illustration of the fact that nothing is hidden from the eyes of Him with whom we have to do. Ezekiel was permitted to look into a central chamber in the temple. Entering the door, he saw a shocking sight. There were the elders of Israel. Heavy incense enveloped them and they were doing obeisance to creeping things, abominable beasts, and the vile symbols of idolatry scribbled on the wall.

What a vivid phrase the Lord used in showing the prophet the significance of this sight! "Hast thou seen," He said, "what the ancients of the house of Israel do in the dark, every man in the chambers of his imagery" (v. 12). "The chambers of his imagery." These are words not readily forgotten, for they ask us about what is going on in the inner places of our lives, in the depths of our hearts.

AUGUST 8

Oh, that I might have my request; and that God would grant me the thing that I long for! (JOB 6:8).

What was Job's request? What was it he was longing for? The next verse gives the answer: "Even that it would please God to destroy me." Death was the thing Job was pleading for.

What a loss to the world it would have been, had that request of Job's been answered! Undoubtedly he was praying with all his might. But insistent though his prayer was, it was not answered. Had death come to Job at that point in his life, the world would never have had the example of his suffering, for the great book bearing his name would never have been written. That Job was required to go on and live is an evidence of the divine wisdom.

Who can estimate the importance to God and man of those brave souls who come through fiery trial to victory! Your struggle may be hidden from human eyes. It may never be written down in a book, as was Job's experience. Nevertheless, it is important to God and, in ways you cannot even begin to realize, to your fellow man also.

AUGUST 9

Everyone who commits sin also commits lawlessness (1 JOHN 3:4, Weymouth).

Among the virtues of this epistle is the way it calls things by their right names. We abhor lawlessness. Technically virtuous, many of us Christians look in horror upon the transgressor against society. But how shocked we should be to realize that we too are lawless, that our very pride in our righteousness is as much sin in God's sight as the crime of the thief or gangster. All sin is transgression of the law of God; every sinner is a spiritual outlaw. Pardon comes only through the mercy of the eternal Judge in accepting in our behalf the perfect obedience of Christ who alone was fully law-abiding. To remember this will help us fulfill our obligation "to do justly, and to love mercy, and to walk humbly with . . . [our] God" (Micah 6:8).

AUGUST 10

Now the God of peace, that brought again from the dead our Lord Jesus, that great shepherd of the sheep, through the blood of the everlasting covenant . . . (HEBREWS 13:20).

"The blood of the everlasting covenant." This is the link between Christ's death and His rising from the grave. He died as a ransom for our sins. He rose for our justification. Had His death been any other but the death of the divine sin-bearer, He would have remained in the grave. And had He, after those hours of suffering on the cross, been held under the power of death, there would have been no redemption for any man. Paul spoke truly, "If Christ be not raised, your faith is vain; ye are yet in your sins" (1 Corinthians 15:17).

We see, therefore, that the two—His death and His rising again—are inextricably united. And what unites them is "the blood of the everlasting covenant." When our Lord gave His life on Calvary, He sealed with His own blood the covenant of grace. That covenant expressed the divine will. Sealed by the blood, it was ratified by the Resurrection. For every believer the conflict between God's righteousness and sin's rebellion is over because of what the God of peace has done through our Lord Jesus, that great Shepherd of the sheep.

AUGUST 11

For whosoever shall do the will of God, the same is my brother, and my sister, and mother (MARK 3:35).

In these words our Lord tells how to be very near to Him. Have you ever thought that admiration and devotion and worship, though all very fitting and necessary, are not by themselves sufficient to bring us close to the Lord? We may practice them all and yet be far from Christ, if we lack the practical requirement of doing the will of God.

Think of being as close to Christ as His own brother and sister and—we hardly dare voice the thought—His mother! Yet He Himself assures us that this may actually be our position in relation to Him, if we are doing the will of God. Religious ecstasy fails, but simple obedience succeeds in bringing us near the Lord Jesus.

AUGUST 12

And the Lord said unto Cain, Where is Abel thy brother? And he said, I know not: Am I my brother's keeper? (GENESIS 4:9).

Cain, having slain Abel, heard God ask, "Where is Abel thy brother?" He answered with the counter question, "Am I my brother's keeper?" In this way the first murderer tried to evade his crime. But God cannot be put off with rhetorical questions. Cain became a marked man as God dealt with his sin.

But let us look at Cain's question in its larger application. To this attempted evasion of responsibility there is only one answer. We are all the keepers of our brothers. We must have respect for the welfare of others. The attitude of heartless unconcern for one's fellow man that was characteristic of Cain is a prime factor in the sufferings of our time. The Gospel brings individual salvation. But it also has its social implications. We who have received eternal life in Christ must not only realize that we are our brothers' keepers in respect to their souls' salvation, but we must also embody our concern for them in loving ministry to their physical needs.

AUGUST 13

They brought forth the sick into the streets, and laid them on beds and couches, that at least the shadow of Peter passing by might overshadow some of them (ACTS 5:15).

A man's shadow is the natural type of his influence. And the question for each of us is this: What kind of spiritual shadow do you cast; what kind of influence do you exercise? For it is a law of the spiritual life that you can no more escape radiating an influence than you can evade casting a physical shadow. It is the light behind and above you that makes your shadow. And it is the illumination behind your life that forms your spiritual shadow of influence. Make sure that you are walking in the true light of Christ, the Sun of Righteousness, and your shadow will be a helpful one like that of Peter.

AUGUST 14

"Take away the stone!" Jesus ordered (JOHN 11:39, TEV).

Jesus knew exactly what He was going to do. He knew that, apart from His divine power, Lazarus would certainly remain in that tomb. He knew that no force on earth aside from His sovereign Word could call His friend out of the grave. He was fully aware that Lazarus was forever beyond the help of Mary or Martha or of the bystanders. Yet Jesus also knew that there was something those bystanders could do. So He asked them, as a preliminary to the miracle, to do it. "Take away the stone!" He commanded them. If we read on, we see that Martha, so trusting yet so practical-minded, remonstrated with the Lord. But her objection was overruled and the stone removed.

There come times in our lives when we realize that nothing short of God's own power can help us. If we are to go on, we need Him to act in our behalf. Yet sometimes He first asks us to "take away the stone." He has in mind some preliminary that is within our power and that is a token of our full reliance upon Him. Though it is only speculation, we can hardly help wondering whether Lazarus would ever have been raised if no one had obeyed Christ in taking away the stone. When Christ tells us to take away some stone in our lives, then we must obey Him.

AUGUST 15

They returned again to Lystra, and to Iconium, and Antioch (Acts 14:21b).

This is the record of a very courageous piece of service. At Lystra, Paul had been stoned and dragged out of the city for dead. And while he and Barnabas were at Iconium and Antioch there had been dangerous riots. Yet to those very places they returned and strengthened the disciples with the exhortation "that we must through much tribulation enter into the kingdom of God" (v. 22). If ever preaching was backed by the life, this was. Enduring advances for God are made, not by evading the places of temporary defeat in our lives, but by returning to them and transforming, under God, the setbacks into victories.

You and I have our Lystras, Iconiums, and Antiochs. Let us trust God for strength, not to detour around them, but to face them and turn them by faith into victories for Him.

AUGUST 16

And all things, whatsoever ye shall ask in prayer, believing, ye shall receive (Matthew 21:22).

The vital word in this promise is certainly the word "believing." Prayer has in it more than asking. It goes beyond worship. Prayer to be effectual must be vitalized by the element of belief. Otherwise it rises no higher than repetition of pious words.

Consider for a moment the monstrosity of unbelieving prayer. How can any reasonable person expect God to take seriously a petition he himself does not even believe will come to pass? Of what value is prayer devoid of some nucleus of faith? At best it is a mere form of words, perhaps beautiful and eloquent, but lifeless, because the speaker does not really believe his prayer will be acted upon by the Giver of all good things.

Faith is the key that opens the doors of God's promises. "And all things whatsoever ye shall ask in prayer, believing, ye shall receive." May God grant us the gift of faith for our prayer life.

AUGUST 17

For them that honour me I will honour, and they that despise me shall be lightly esteemed (1 SAMUEL 2:30b).

These words come to us through an anonymous prophet who spoke to Eli. They set forth the spiritual principle that honoring God brings blessing, while despising Him brings sorrow and ruin.

But how are we to honor God today? In the answer to this question our response to the Gospel is implicit. For God sent His Son, the Lord Jesus Christ, into the world. Just as honoring a monarch's ambassador means honoring the king, so to honor Christ is to honor God. But no one can honor God and at the same time reject His Son, who came to reconcile the world to **His** Father. Rejecting Christ is the essence of despising God, and those who do that have no claim on God's esteem. Have you honored God by receiving His Son? Are you honoring him by obeying His commands? (John 15:14).

AUGUST 18

For he spake, and it was done; he commanded, and it stood fast (PSALM 33:9).

We sometimes say of a man in a position of great authority, "His word is law." Only in a limited sense is this true of any one, no matter how great. But there is One whose Word actually and fully *is* law. That One is the Lord. When He speaks, it is done. What He commands stands fast for ever. Think of creation. God spoke and the world came into being. He spoke again and yet again, and in succession the whole procession of life was called into existence. This ability to create by a word is the prerogative of Deity alone.

No man was present at the creation. No man heard that sublime declaration, "Let there be light" (Genesis 1:3), nor did anyone see the light blaze forth at this word of God. Yet everyone of us who is saved through faith in Christ has experienced the full power of God's utterance. When we were lost in the darkness of sin, He spoke to our hearts by His Word. That Word brought forth in us the light of a new life in Christ. Dark though this world is, we who believe are in the light. Let us, therefore, do as the beloved disciple says and "walk in the light, as he is in the light" (1 John 1:7).

AUGUST 19

And there was a calm. And he said unto them, Where is your faith? (LUKE 8:24b, 25).

Despite their peril on the stormy sea, the disciples might have enjoyed calm in their hearts. Jesus was with them in the ship. They had seen His wonder-working power. But they allowed themselves to be mastered by fear. All this is implied in His gentle rebuke, "Where is your faith?"

How like them we are. Storms are certain to attend our voyage through life. Dangerous winds will beat on us to blow us from our course. But be the tempest ever so fierce, we never once need be mastered by fear. Just think! The Lord is in the ship with us; the Captain of our salvation is charting our course. He would have us be calm within our hearts, trusting Him to rebuke the wind and the waves that threaten our safety.

AUGUST 20

Where is the promise of his coming? for since the fathers fell asleep, all things continue as they were from the beginning of the creation (2 PETER 3:4).

One of the commonest arguments of the modern skeptic is based on uniformitarianism. There can, he says, be nothing supernatural in the Christian faith; miracles cannot have occurred in the past because nature is uniform. Any intervention in the natural course of events is therefore ruled out. But nineteen hundred years ago Peter anticipated this argument. "There shall," he wrote, "come in the last days scoffers . . . saying, Where is the promise of His coming? for since the fathers fell asleep all things continue as they were since the beginning of the creation" (vv. 3, 4). Then he proceeded (vv. 5, 6, 7) to refer to the unbelievers' willful ignorance of God's stupendous intervention in nature through the flood, and continued with the assurance that "one day is with the Lord as a thousand years, and a thousand years as one day" (v. 8).

The God who intervened through the flood will yet send His Son from heaven. The promise of His coming is as sure as His Word. Though the enemy seems victorious and sin triumphant God does have the last word. Christ is coming!

AUGUST 21

And seekest thou great things for thyself? seek them not
(JEREMIAH 45:5).

Jeremiah, who of all the major prophets had the least public
acclaim, must have found comfort in this message given him
through his secretary, Baruch. It must have helped him when
he had to stand alone in the last days of Jerusalem proclaiming
over and over again an unwelcome and bitter message. It must
have been a solace to this sorely tested prophet to know that
God had said expressly to him, "And seekest thou great things
for thyself? seek them not."

So universally true are these words that we may take them
to heart without the slightest change. Never is it in accord
with God's highest purpose for His children that they seek
great things just for themselves. To be sure, great things may
come to us, but they will come as a by-product, not as the result
of self-seeking. Whenever ambition seeks to dominate us, then
we should ask ourselves the plain question, "Seekest thou great
things for thyself?" And as we ask that question, we shall hear
God's answer, which is always the same, "Seek them not."

AUGUST 22

*Therefore being justified by faith, we have peace with
God through our Lord Jesus Christ* (ROMANS 5:1).

Drawing to the close of his great exposition of justification
by faith, Paul pauses to list some of its results, the first of these
being peace with God. Let us mark the preposition, for it is important. This is not that subjective peace "of" God which Paul
mentions elsewhere, but an objective peace, signalizing the cessation of hostility between man and God. Man is naturally the
enemy of God, for man is sinful and God is eternally opposed to
sin. But justification, being the full acquittal of the sinner because of the imputed righteousness of Christ, brings lasting
peace with God. That is the essential basis of the Christian life,
the secure foundation that can never be moved. Paul does not
say we have peace with God through the church, or through the
sacraments, or through confirmation, or any other religious or-
dinance. But he does say "we have peace with God through our
Lord Jesus Christ."

Are you trusting Christ and Him alone for your salvation?
Then you have an unchallengeable right to this "peace with
God."

AUGUST 23

Ponder the path of thy feet (PROVERBS 4:26).

Doubtless most readers of these daily messages use them in the mornings. But today let us consider a Scripture that, while having a meaning for the morning, is peculiarly applicable to the end of the day. "Ponder the path of thy feet." Try it tonight, on your knees, alone with God. Review your steps of the day, the places you went and what you did. Let Him speak to you and teach you out of your own experience during this day.

And for the morning? Well, you know that you can't ponder the path of your feet even one day in advance. God alone knows where you will go and all you will do. So step forth each day, committing your way to Him in faith.

AUGUST 24

If that nation, against whom I have pronounced, turn from their evil, I will repent of the evil that I thought to do unto them. . . . If it do evil in my sight, that it obey not my voice, then I will repent of the good, wherewith I said I would benefit them (JEREMIAH 18:8, 10).

It was in the potter's house, as Jeremiah was watching the swiftly turning wheel, that the Lord spoke these words to him. It is true that God is the potter and we are the clay. But it is not true that we are mere insentient clay and that, regardless of what we do, our lives are fatalistically predetermined. Quite the contrary, such a view of the divine dealing with men is repudiated in this passage. "If," said the Lord to Jeremiah, "a nation turn from their evil," or "if it do evil in my sight" (having previously done good), "then," the Lord continued, "I will repent of this evil that I thought to do unto them" or "then I will repent of the good." In either case God's final action takes into account the moral choice of man.

Each day we live has its relation to God's eternal purpose for us. Each may be marked by some definite moral choice we make according to our human will. Nor may we Christians hide from responsibility in the thought that we are children of God. The Heavenly Father must discipline His children no less than an earthly father.

AUGUST 25

Yet to all who received him, to those who believed in his name, he gave the right to become children of God (JOHN 1:12, NIV).

For many this verse has been the doorway to everlasting life. Christianity, it shows us, is first of all Christ. Being a child of God is the result of receiving a person. The method of receiving Him is by believing on His name.

Now if only those who receive the Lord Jesus by believing on His name are children of God, it must follow that all others are not God's children. This is one of the most vital distinctions in Scripture. But how often it is overlooked! We are prone to blur the distinction between the children of God and the children of the world. Though by creation we are all God's offspring, only those who have received Christ in their hearts by faith are His children in Christ. Let us not take our neighbors and friends for granted, but let us, as opportunity affords, show them how to enter into the fellowship of God's children.

AUGUST 26

And there has not arisen a prophet since in Israel like Moses, whom the Lord knew face to face (DEUTERONOMY 34:10, RSV).

This is a portion of Moses' epitaph. The first thing said of him, the thing that takes precedence over the signs and wonders (vv. 11, 12) he did in Egypt, is the fact that the Lord knew him face to face. The heart of Moses' towering greatness lay in his nearness to God. Remember how, when Moses returned from Sinai, he had to veil his face because of the glory shining from it.

But we Christians have in store for us an even closer fellowship with the Lord than Moses had. Says the beloved disciple in a passage applying to every believer: "When he [Christ] shall appear, we shall be like him; for we shall see him as he is" (1 John 3:2). One day, as surely as sunset follows dawn, the Lord Jesus will return, and then we shall see Him face to face. That moment of recognition will change us into His glorious likeness. So let us consider how we ought to live here and now. For as John goes on to say, "Everyone who thus hopes in him purifies himself as he is pure (1 John 3:3, RSV).

AUGUST 27

If anyone lets himself be dominated by anything, then he is a slave to it (2 PETER 2:19, JB).

This forthright statement gives us pause. Slavery is not dead. While human beings may no longer be sold in civilized countries, their souls, and their bodies too, are still subject to slavery. Bondage to drink or gluttony, to lust or drugs is slavery. But Peter used the word "anything." Do we realize that, if we are habitually overcome by temper, depression, hatred, prejudice, or selfishness, we are just as surely enslaved as the drunkard or drug addict?

But there is a way out. Thanks be unto God for freedom from slavery to sin through repentance and faith in Christ's redeeming work on Calvary!

AUGUST 28

They sang the song of Moses the servant of God, and the song of the Lamb:

> *"Great and marvelous are your deeds*
> *Lord God Almighty.*
> *Just and true are your ways,*
> *King of the ages.*
> *Who will not fear you, O Lord,*
> *And bring glory to your name?*
> *You alone are holy.*
> *All nations will come and worship before you,*
> *Your righteous acts have been revealed."*
> (REVELATION 15:3, 4, NIV).

What honor this song confers upon Moses by linking his name with the Lamb! It is the essence of true worship. It is great in its ascription of praise. Sung from the side of eternity, it acknowledges the perfection of God's works. What we now see by faith, it celebrates out of the knowledge of heaven where all is made manifest and the marvels of God's dealings with men are fully revealed. So let us acknowledge the greatness and wonder of God's works, the justice and truth of His ways. Let us fear Him and glorify His Name, because He alone is holy, and all nations shall worship before Him in the day of His judgments. He is the Lord God Almighty, the King of saints. Let us bow down and worship Him.

AUGUST 29

Pray for us (HEBREWS 13:8a).

This is a universal appeal. Over and over again it has arisen from Christians in peril and trial. Let us think of it, as it reaches our ears today. "Pray for us." Consider the many Christians who are facing problems, bearing burdens, suffering illness or bereavement, and who need prayer.

But this exhortation has an even wider application. Think of those who, although they may not be saying "pray for us," are yet making this plea. They do not know Christ. And therefore the very emptiness of their hearts is a silent prayer for our supplication in their behalf. Surely we need not go on. The whole lost world is crying out to us who know the way to the throne of grace, "Pray for us." How can we let a single day go by without spending some time in intercession!

AUGUST 30

Consecrate yourselves therefore, and be holy; for I am the Lord your God. Keep my statutes, and do them; I am the Lord who sanctify you (LEVITICUS 20:7, 8, RSV).

Leviticus is a great Old Testament source for the doctrine of sanctification. Throughout its pages holiness to the Lord is stressed. Apart from this great concept, the sacrifices, offerings, and all the laws relating to the life of God's people can hardly be understood.

Now in the passage before us we have two essential aspects of sanctification. "Consecrate yourself"—this is the human side of this great doctrine. "I am the Lord who sanctify you"—that is its divine side. What is here set down so tersely by Moses is elaborated in the New Testament. Particularly in Paul's treatment of the subject, as in Romans 6, 7, 8, we recognize the twofold aspect of sanctification. It is a matter of Christian experience and therefore relates to self-surrender to the indwelling Christ. Yet it is also a matter of faith and not of works; for when a believer yields himself wholly to Christ, he realizes that Christ has indeed made full provision for his sanctification. And he also knows that scriptural holiness is to be appropriated by faith and is to be lived through moment by moment trust in the risen Lord

AUGUST 31

Just as Moses lifted up the serpent in the wilderness, so the Son of man must be lifted up, so that whoever believes in him may not perish but have life eternal (JOHN 3:14, 15, Berkeley).

This is one of the more difficult of our Lord's comparisons. For how could the Son of man, spotless in His sinless perfection, be likened to the serpent, the symbol of sin? How could the Lord Jesus compare Himself, the Saviour, with the serpent? And compare them He does; if language means anything at all, the Saviour and the serpent are explicitly linked in this remarkable verse.

The answer to this difficulty brings us to the deep things of our redemption. As He uttered these words, Jesus was thinking of the time when disobedient Israel, wandering in the wilderness, was punished by the scourge of venomous serpents. It was then that, as Israel cried out for mercy, the Lord commanded Moses to set a serpent of bronze upon a pole that all who looked to it might live (Numbers 21:5-9). Now that bronze serpent had in it no venom, but it represented the poisonous serpents that were afflicting the people. So our Lord, hanging upon Calvary's cross, had in Him no sin, yet the sins of all humanity were placed on Him. Even more, He was at that time identified with the sin of the world, with your sin and mine. As Paul wonderfully put it, "God made him who knew no sin to be made sin in our behalf, so that in him we might share the righteousness of God" (2 Corinthians 5:21, Berkeley).

Yes, the type is complete. But is it complete in you? There is one thing the dying Israelites had to do in order to have life; they had to look to the serpent nailed to the pole. So everyone who believes in the crucified Saviour may have eternal life. Have you looked in faith to the Son of man, nailed to the cross for you? Are you continuing to look to Him for victory over the sin that so easily besets us?

SEPTEMBER 1

*The One who started the good work in you will bring it to
completion by the Day of Christ Jesus* (PHILIPPIANS 1:6,
NEB).

There are several reasons why these words are appropriate
today. For one thing, they place the emphasis wholly upon God.
Just what blessings may be ours this month we know not. But
this we do know: everything good we shall receive or do will
have its source in God and not in us.

Also we find in these words an encouraging principle, for
Paul assures us that He who has blessed us in the past will perfect what He has begun. Every single blessing of past days
is a sure token of the continuance of His benevolence; each
good thing He has already done in and through us is a pledge
of His future kindness. The same God who saved us by His
grace will carry us through to our completion in Christ! Let
us, therefore, go on with confidence in the ability of the divine
Initiator of every blessing to complete the work He has begun
in us.

SEPTEMBER 2

*The voice of the Lord is upon the waters; the God of glory
thundereth; the Lord is upon many waters* (PSALM 29:3).

This twenty-ninth psalm might well be entitled "The Thun-
derstorm." It portrays the power of God shown in the terror
of a great storm. But we must go deeper than literary appreciation of this vivid psalm. Only eleven verses comprise it, but six-
teen times in these eleven verses we read the words, "The Lord."
In the awe-inspiring storm David saw God. For the sweet singer
of Israel, God was in every thundercloud, terrible though it was.
He was in each flash of lightning, and in all the turmoil of wind
and water. God is in our storms as well as in the quiet places of
our lives. Let us learn to see Him everywhere, knowing that He
is in and above every storm that breaks upon our lives, giving
strength to His people and working out His purpose to bless
them with His peace (v. 11).

SEPTEMBER 3

You were called unto the fellowship of his Son (1 CORIN-THIANS 1:9).

Fellowship is reciprocal. Where one person is active and the other only passive, there can be no continuing fellowship. Active interchange is essential to it.

Remember, then, that God has called us Christians into that kind of relationship, into real fellowship with His Son. He means for us to talk with Him, to walk with Him, daily to seek His approval and His guidance. Christ wants us to serve actively in the yoke of fellowship with Himself. We are to be partners in His work of love and compassion. For what He said to His first disciples—"As my Father has sent me, even so send I you" (John 20:21)—applies also to us.

SEPTEMBER 4

And this is the confidence which we have before him, that, if we ask anything according to his will, he hears us (1 JOHN 5:14, NASV).

"This is the confidence which we have before Him, that he hears us." That, however, is not what John wrote. No, he inserted a conditional clause, "if we ask anything according to his will." If we do this, if we ask according to His will, God will hear us.

This condition points back to our Lord's own practice of prayer. As He agonized in Gethsemane, He wholly accepted as the great basis of prayer, "Thy will be done" (Matthew 26:42b). Though it cost Him the anguish of great drops of blood, though it led Him to the cross and the grave, He submitted Himself to the Father's will. And how clearly He was vindicated in His choice! His resurrection and ascension are the eternal demonstration of the victory that follows full submission to the will of God.

Yes, we may ask anything of God in prayer; there is nothing we may not bring before Him. But we must be willing for our requests to be dealt with in God's own way and according to His own perfect will. When we identify with Christ's submission in Gethsemane, "Not my will, but thine, be done" (Luke 22:42), then we may be confident that God hears us.

SEPTEMBER 5

Use hospitality one to another without grudging (1 PETER 4:9).

Hospitality is just one example of the many virtues that grudging can ruin. But what is grudging? It is the attitude of heart that says, "Oh, well, I guess I'll have to do this kind act." Grudging is niggardly. It comes from a spirit that does good and bestows praise more because it has to than because it wants to, a spirit that is too small to overflow in spontaneous kindness. It is the selfish counterfeit of the benevolence that wells up in a heart devoted to Christ.

When grudging taints our good impulses and gracious acts, we may be perfectly certain that self in our lives is usurping the place belonging to the Lord alone. Grudging is sin because it goes back to self, and self is the fertile soil where sin flourishes.

SEPTEMBER 6

And the Spirit and the bride say, Come. And let him that heareth say, Come. And let him that is athirst come. And whosoever will, let him take the water of life freely (REVELATION 22:17).

"Come" is a characteristic word of the conclusion of the book of Revelation. The Holy Spirit and the bride of Christ, which is the Church, unite in this great evangelical word. "Come," they say. To everyone who hears the Word of God, they proclaim, "Come." To all who are hungering and thirsting after righteousness they cry, "Come." And then they add, "Whosoever will, let him take the water of life freely."

From beginning to end the Bible is concerned with our spiritual need. Its invitation is essentially a personal one. Have you who are reading these words accepted that invitation? You personally are bidden to receive new life in Christ. For to come to Him is to turn away from any thought of salvation through your own righteousness and to trust in Him as your only Saviour and Lord. Have you come to "take the water of life freely"?

SEPTEMBER 7

But truly I am full of power by the Spirit of the Lord, and of judgment, and of might, to declare unto Jacob his transgression, and to Israel his sin (MICAH 3:8).

Sometimes we are called to the very difficult ministry of rebuke. To speak about transgressions of others takes something more than the courage it certainly requires. It takes nothing less than the power and compassion of the Holy Spirit. If you are ever in a place where you are called upon to administer a serious rebuke, make sure that, prayerfully and humbly, you have first of all sought the guidance and strengthening of the Spirit of the Lord.

SEPTEMBER 8

My soul shall make her boast in the Lord: the humble shall hear thereof, and be glad (PSALM 34:2).

Why is it that David followed his declaration of boasting in the Lord by this statement about the humble? Why did he say that the humble shall be glad? Well, when eminent men boast of their own greatness, their boasting may be discouraging to those about them. What encouragement is it for a citizen to have a boasting ruler, proud in his own strength? The citizen has little hope of becoming a great ruler. What good is it for the poor to hear the self-congratulation of some millionaire? The poor know they will never have such riches. Not only is such boasting, whether of men or nations, discouraging; it is also perilous to the humble, for it may fill his heart with the bitterness of frustration.

How different was the example of David! Here was a man called to rule over God's people. He had pre-eminent ability and true greatness. But he put all this aside, and resolved to boast only in the Lord. That was the kind of acclaim that made the humble rejoice, for they could follow such a leader. They too could join in praising the Lord, who is so infinitely above even the greatest of rulers. Self-praise never satisfies anyone, but praising God nourishes and gladdens the heart.

SEPTEMBER 9

The Lord is good, a strong hold in the day of trouble; and he knoweth them that trust in him (NAHUM 1:7).

"He knoweth them that trust in him." There is a wealth of comfort and strength in these words. The hours of each new day are a journey into the unknown. Should they bring sudden sorrow, unexpected difficulty, or misunderstanding even of your purest motives, then rest, Christian friend, in the fact that the Lord knows what man can never fully know. He *knows* with infallible certainty those who are really trusting in Him. And that is enough for your solace and your reassurance.

SEPTEMBER 10

Every man shall give as he is able, according to the blessing of the Lord thy God which he hath given thee (DEUTERONOMY 16:17).

Here is a rule for giving. First, it says that "every man" is to give. We recognize, of course, that Moses gave this rule to Israel. The call was not for gifts from the world; it was only His people who were addressed. But for them there was no exception; all were included. Then the verse goes on to tell about the extent of giving. No set amount was here prescribed. To do so would have been unjust to the poor and inadequate for the rich. Therefore all were to give as the Lord had prospered them.

Although this is an Old Testament text, its meaning is timeless. It goes with what Paul wrote about giving as God has prospered us (1 Corinthians 16:1, 2) and also with his words in 2 Corinthians 8:12, "Provided there is an eager desire to give, God accepts what a man has; he does not ask for what he has not" (NEB). Giving according to biblical principles is an integral part of our witness; and to give generously to the Lord is a happy experience we all can have regardless of the size of our resources (Mark 12:41-44).

SEPTEMBER 11

God is not a man, that he should lie; neither the son of man, that he should repent; hath he said, and shall he not do it? or hath he spoken, and shall he not make it good? (NUMBERS 23:19).

. Here is stability. God can always be depended upon. Unlike man it is impossible for Him to lie. Not only that, but He does not fluctuate either in His words or acts. When God says a thing, it will be done. What He promises, He makes good.

So this statement given by God to that strange prophet, Balaam, teaches us to accept the commitments of our Lord with wholehearted faith. It reminds us of His utter consistency. Believing in this God of all reliability, let us not hesitate to accept the hundreds of precious promises in Scripture. God never changes. He does what He says; He makes good every pledge He gives us in His Word.

SEPTEMBER 12

Woe unto thee, Chorazin! woe unto thee, Bethsaida! for if the mighty works, which were done in you, had been done in Tyre and Sidon, they would have repented long ago in sackcloth and ashes (MATTHEW 11:21).

What were the mighty works done in Chorazin and Bethsaida? The answer points to Christ's ministry, including His miracles. These manifestations of grace, He said, would have caused even Tyre and Sidon to repent.

Now our Lord is still doing mighty works. Every time a soul is saved, every time a prayer is answered, every time the way is prepared for the Lord's people—that is a mighty work. Every evidence of divine grace in our behalf is a work of our Lord. Chorazin and Bethsaida faced judgment because they did not repent at Christ's mighty works. But how is it with us? Does each mighty work of the Lord in our behalf—that answered prayer, that spiritual blessing, that opened door of service—increase our repentance?

Repentance means a changed mind. God's goodness to us should lead to renewed awareness of our helpless condition apart from Christ. It should make us thankful for every blessing we enjoy. For to take God's mercies for granted is incompatible with our repentance.

SEPTEMBER 13

Our lips are our own (PSALM 12:4).

So man speaks in his willful pride. But they are not; his lips are not his own. They were made by God; God knows every word that issues from them. God holds their possessor as accountable for his words as He does for the deeds of his hands. Sometimes words *are* deeds. And the one who says, "My lips are my own," is foolish. Rather than claiming exclusive ownership of our lips, we should be praying as David did in the Nineteenth Psalm: "Let the words of my mouth . . . be acceptable in thy sight, O Lord, my strength, and my redeemer."

SEPTEMBER 14

And the devil said unto him, All this power will I give thee, and the glory of them: for that is delivered unto me; and to whomsoever I will I give it (LUKE 4:6).

If the devil could say to Christ, "All this power will I give thee . . . for that is delivered unto me; and to whomsoever I will I give it," and say it, as he did, with reference to "all the kingdoms of the world" (v. 5); then we may conclude that Satan is behind human plans for world conquest. To those who, having left out God, look upon this world as man's exclusive province, this is a radical thought. Yet not only here but elsewhere the New Testament teaches that Satan controls the present world order—not the physical world, but the world system, "the kingdoms of the world." Our Lord Himself called Satan "the prince of this world" (John 14:30). Let us Christians be careful, therefore, never to pin our hopes on any merely human dream of world conquest—yes, even the dream of democracy. For democracy without Christ is not enough.

Some will call this pessimistic. But Scripture is not pessimistic—not in its ultimate issue. We have only to go back to the context of our verse for today. The devil tempted Christ, but Christ vanquished him. So let us remember that there is surely coming the day of consummation, when the "kingdoms of this world," having been wrested from the grip of their prince, will "become the kingdoms of our Lord, and of his Christ; and he shall reign for ever and ever" (Revelation 11:15).

SEPTEMBER 15

The Father loveth the Son, and hath given all things into his hand (JOHN 3:35).

Whatever you may be facing, whatever may happen, take this sentence as the basis of your assurance for this day. The Father is all-knowing as well as all-powerful. Surely He knows best, surely He knows that His dear Son is fully trustworthy! Yes, the Father loves the Son, and proves His love by committing "all things into His hand." O Christian, receive these words at their plain, face value. "All things" include you and everything that pertains to you. You are in the hands of the Lord Jesus. If God the Father was willing to entrust the universe to Him, should you be hesitant about giving all you have and are and hope to be into His own hand?

SEPTEMBER 16

Let him that stole steal no more: but rather let him labour, working with his hands the thing which is good, that he may have to give to him that needeth (EPHESIANS 4:28).

Paul knew that the most common motive for theft is the covetous desire for something belonging to another. He realized that almost all stealing stems from selfishness. So he prescribed work for an altruistic purpose as the remedy for dishonesty: "working with his hands the thing which is good, that he may have to give to him that needeth."

We may never have stolen money, but there are few of us not guilty of stealing time. The time of our working hours belongs to our employer; the rest is ours. So most of us say. But back of it all for us Christians is the fact that every minute of our time belongs to God. The common expression, "to steal a moment," points to dishonesty in relation to time. What are we doing when we waste an hour over a book or picture that combines worthlessness with depravity? Are we honest with God when we spend in sin the moments He has given us, even in such a "little" sin as gossip? Useful work for the benefit of others is one of God's medicines for healing the deviousness to which we are all prone. May we learn to take more of this medicine!

SEPTEMBER 17

And [I] shall put my spirit in you, and ye shall live (EZE-
KIEL 37:14a).

This is the only way in which anybody can know God. The
human spirit is so ruined in sin as to be incapable by itself of
vital contact with its Maker. It may **seem** drastic to say this,
but it is nevertheless true that, until God works a miracle in
the human heart, there can be no true fellowship with Him.
Once realized, this basic spiritual fact does away with all pride
of religion. It excludes all formalism that seeks to approach God
through human means alone, and it reveals the error of a mysticism that depends on the unregenerate human spirit for contact
with the divine. If it is true that we live spiritually only when
God puts His Spirit within us, then there is no place for pride
in religious attainment. The very life in which we worship God
and serve Him is the gift of His grace. To acknowledge this is
the beginning of the humility or poverty of spirit that Jesus
called blessed (Matthew 5:3).

SEPTEMBER 18

*And the Lord said unto Noah, Come thou and all thy
house into the ark; for thee have I seen righteous before me
in this generation* (GENESIS 7:1).

Here for the first time in Scripture God used the word
'Come" in an invitational sense. Noah, obedient to the divine
command, had prepared the ark. Judgment threatened the
earth. Then God said to Noah, "Come thou and all thy house
into the ark." And He went on to say why Noah was invited
into this place of safety: "For thee have I seen righteous before
me in this generation."

God's invitation for Noah and his household to come to
the one refuge from impending wrath was given on the basis
of righteousness. But we must recognize that God spoke to Noah
in grace and not on any ground of human merit. Like all men,
Noah was, as his later life showed, a sinner. Yet he believed
what God said about building the ark. And because he believed
and acted accordingly, God counted his faith for righteousness.

God is still saying "Come." Through His grace He continues
to bring sinners into that spiritual ark, which is Christ. And
how is He saying "Come"? Well, one of the ways He is saying
it is when we invite others to come to our Lord. Essential to the
vocabulary of Christian witness is the word "Come."

SEPTEMBER 19

The thought of foolishness is sin (PROVERBS 24:9).

Here Solomon probes into the roots of sin. He is pointing out that it is not in the act of folly that the sin lies but in the preliminary thought of folly. This precept is profoundly true psychologically as well as spiritually. Thoughts are not light things. They are important, for they tend to action. And thoughts of folly, when harbored and indulged, surely bear fruit in acts of folly.

Can there be a more necessary prayer for us who desire to live lives well-pleasing to God than this: "O God, guard my thoughts today. Bring every one of them into captivity to the obedience of Christ!"

SEPTEMBER 20

Holiness befits thy house, O Lord, for evermore. (PSALM 93:5, RSV).

This psalm compresses a maximum of praise into a minimum of words. Only five verses long, it fairly sings with the glory of the Lord. And this final sentence applies to us.

"Holiness becometh thine house forever." Granted that the word "house" refers first of all to the temple, the term has a broader reference. All who name the name of Christ comprise the household of faith. All who are regenerated are built up into a spiritual house to the honor of Him who is the Chief Cornerstone (1 Peter 2:5-8). Moreover Peter, who so beautifully expresses this thought, reminds us in the same epistle of the obligation of sanctification by quoting the Levitical word, "Ye shall be holy; for I am holy" (Leviticus 11:44).

Oh, that every one of us believers might realize that nothing is more essential than a holy life! For this quality in the Christian there can be no substitute. "But," say some, "we ourselves are so very far from holiness." That is true. And it is also true that holiness is never achieved merely by self-effort. Long ago a great saint said, "If I were given the power to work miracles, I would ask only the miracle of a holy life." In this sinful world, holiness is nothing short of miraculous. But it is a miracle God loves to work, and keep on working, in response to our daily commitment of self—body, soul, and mind—to the Saviour.

SEPTEMBER 21

And, lo, the heavens were opened unto him (MATTHEW 3:16).

Let the baptism of our Lord remind us today that He opened heaven for sinners. After He came out of the water "the heavens were opened unto him." So His life on earth was lived in constant communion with the Father above. And finally after His resurrection He was received up into heaven for eternal communion with the Father.

By God's grace we may relate these things to ourselves. Christ died for our sins and rose again for our justification. Through Him Christians are brought into fellowship with the Father. To us who have been baptized into His death and who have risen into a new life in Him the heavens are also open. Very wonderfully does Paul develop this truth in Ephesians, where he reminds us of our present position in the heavenly places (Ephesians 1:3). So let us be diligent to walk worthy of our high calling in Christ Jesus, remembering that, because the heavens were opened to Him, they are also open to us.

SEPTEMBER 22

Take thee again another roll, and write in it all the former words that were in the first roll, which Jehoiakim the king of Judah hath burned (JEREMIAH 36:28).

In accordance with the express command of God, Jeremiah had dictated to Baruch the message God gave him, and Baruch had written it down upon a scroll. But the message was hateful to Jehoiakim and his princes. Therefore when it was read to him, King Jehoiakim took the scroll containing the Word of Jehovah, deliberately sliced it to bits with his penknife, and threw it into the flames on the palace hearth. But that act had a sequel. A terrible judgment was pronounced upon Jehoiakim. He was to be killed and his body cast out of the city. "He shall be buried with the burial of an ass, drawn and cast forth beyond the gates of Jerusalem" (Jeremiah 22:19). And as for the Word he thought he had destroyed, it came once more to Jeremiah and was written down again by Baruch the scribe. What an illustration of the psalmist's statement, "For ever, O Lord, thy word is settled in heaven" (Psalm 119:89)! God's Word is indestructible and no one disregards it with impunity.

SEPTEMBER 23

Thou calledst in trouble, and I delivered thee; I answered thee in the secret place of thunder (PSALM 81:7).

"The secret place of thunder." The figure is striking. It may allude to what happened at Mt. Sinai when the law was given. But there is also a broader interpretation. By "the secret place of thunder" we may think of the times of conflict and turmoil that come to us. Misfortunes, disillusionments, sorrows, and reverses befall us. Adversity threatens us. Then God speaks. In the noise of conflict there is an inner place of calm. Just as there are some ears that are able to distinguish certain soft tones even in the clamor of a steel mill, so some souls are attuned to God's voice in the storms of life. When the thunder comes in your life, listen carefully. God may be speaking to you.

SEPTEMBER 24

"Men of Galilee," they said, "why do you stand there looking up into the sky? This Jesus, who was taken up from you into heaven, will come back in the same way that you saw him go to heaven" (ACTS 1:11, TEV).

This verse assures us of the return of Christ. It was spoken not by men but by angels. The disciples were spellbound as they saw their Lord, who had so recently triumphed over death, taken up into heaven. They could not tear their eyes from the cloud that received Him out of their sight. But they could not always be gazing into heaven, and so the assurance came that their ascended Lord would return. Therefore it was futile for them to keep looking into the sky.

Someone said that, when it comes to belief in the Lord's return, there are two kinds of Christians—gazers and goers. The disciples, momentarily gazers, speedily became goers—yes, even to distant parts of the earth. Being sure of their Lord's coming back, they had no need to keep their eyes fixed on the clouds. Their task was to witness to Him by word and by deed. It is vital for Christians to believe in the Lord's return, but such belief must always be related to witness and service.

SEPTEMBER 25

*But of the fruit of the tree which is in the midst of the
garden, God hath said, Ye shall not eat of it, neither shall
ye touch it, lest ye die. And the serpent said unto the
woman, Ye shall not surely die* (GENESIS 3:3, 4).

Here we see Satan for what he is. Having questioned God's
word to Adam and Eve, he takes the further step of flatly deny-
ing it. Regarding disobedience to His command not to eat of the
tree, God had said to man, "Thou shalt surely die" (2:17).
But Satan said, "Ye shall not surely die."

Many centuries after this record was written, the Lord Jesus
said of Satan, "He is a liar, and the father of it" (John 8:44).
Here, then, is the first lie. Because Eve and her husband believed this lie, sin came into the human race.

Satan never changes; his character remains the same. He is
always at variance with the truth, ever a liar. Thus there is no
form of sin in which we act more satanically than when we indulge in telling a lie. No untruth is ever a little thing; it always
bears the mark of its father, the devil.

SEPTEMBER 26

*A bruised reed shall he not break, and smoking flax shall he
not quench* (MATTHEW 12:20).

Few things are more ineffectual than a bruised reed or a
smoking flax. At its best the reed is pitiably weak and the flax
gives but a poor light. Broken, the reed is useless; smoking, the
flax valueless. And so with us. Disfigured by sin, we are but
broken reeds and smoking flax, yet the Lord Jesus condescends
to treat us with the most tender regard. None of us, no matter
how weak and broken, need ever fear to place himself in
Christ's hands. The touch of those hands is healing and
strengthening. As Dean Alford put it in his *Greek Testament,*
"He will not crush the contrite heart, nor extinguish the slightest spark of repentant feeling in the sinner." Oh, the marvelous
gentleness of our Lord Jesus Christ!

SEPTEMBER 27

He went up into a mountain apart to pray (MATTHEW 14:23).

"He went . . . apart to pray." In this, as in so many other things, He is our perfect example. The Lord Jesus did not neglect public worship in synagogue and temple. But there was always that solitary time of communion. "Apart to pray." Many a Christian life, once powerful and fruitful, is being weakened because of neglect of private prayer. Only those who consistently—day after day, week after week, month after month, and year after year—hold to their daily appointment with God, know the amount of self-discipline it takes to maintain that devotional time. It is not easy, this regular spending of time alone with God every day. But effective Christian service cannot be carried on without it.

SEPTEMBER 28

And Enoch walked with God: and he was not; for God took him (GENESIS 5:24).

"Enoch walked with God." What a marvelous epitome of a holy life! Enoch lived in an evil time when things were heading up to the universal corruption that brought upon humanity the judgment of the flood. Yet in those early years he found grace to walk with God so closely as to be found ready for heaven without passing through the dark river of death. How could this be? The writer of the epistle to the Hebrews gives us the answer: "By faith Enoch was translated" (v. 5). So we see in Enoch the first type of that whole generation of believers who, when the Lord comes, are walking by faith and will be translated from the earthly to the heavenly life (1 Thessalonians 4:13-17).

The return of Christ is an event, said Archbishop Trench, "possible any day, impossible no day." If we take Scripture seriously, we shall be expecting our Lord to come. And if we are looking for Him, we should live so as not to be ashamed of what we are doing when He comes back (1 John 2:28).

SEPTEMBER 29

*Jesus . . . said unto them, Are ye come out, as against a
thief, with swords and with staves to take me? I was daily
with you in the temple teaching, and ye took me not: but
the scriptures must be fulfilled* (MARK 14:48, 49).

It is the dark hour before dawn. An armed band arrests the
Lord Jesus. Peter impetuously cuts off Malchus's ear. The forces
of evil are mounting. Yet against that background the person of
the Lord Jesus stands out in quiet majesty. His very words, as
we read them in our text for today, breathe His calm mastery of
the situation. Murderous hatred seethes in the breasts of His
enemies, violence possesses Peter, but the Lord is calm.

We need to hold before the eyes of our hearts this picture
of our Lord. Life may be turbulent, the enemy may at-
tack with dreadful force and persistency. But the Lord Jesus is
always Master of every situation, and in Him we have inner
security.

SEPTEMBER 30

*The Lord standeth up to plead, and standeth to judge the
people* (ISAIAH 3:13).

Here begins a vivid passage about an obligation neglected by
some Christians. But neither the writers of the Old Testament
nor those of the New Testament overlooked it. The Word of
God lays weighty emphasis upon social justice. Therefore Isaiah
joins with the other inspired authors in representing the Lord as
stirred to holy indignation by injustice and oppression.

Many of us insist that, if the saving Gospel is preached in
power, men will be changed and they will deal with social ills.
But, and the qualification is a large one, let us who cherish the
Gospel and insist on the priority of its proclamation be very
certain that we ourselves have been changed by it to the extent
of being sensitive to the wrongs of the oppressed, the needs of
the afflicted, and the crimes of the unjust. Evangelism and re-
vivals are essential. Yet they do not fulfill our obligation of
godly social concern. The beloved disciple put this obligation
in compelling words when he wrote: "If anyone has material
possessions and sees his brother in need but has no pity on him,
how can the love of God be in him?" (1 John 3:17, NIV).

OCTOBER 1

And it came to pass, that, as he was praying in a certain place, when he ceased, one of the disciples said unto him, Lord, teach us to pray (LUKE 11:1).

It is from Luke alone that we learn that the Lord's Prayer was given in answer to a definite request. Who the disciple was who asked for His teaching on prayer we have no way of knowing. But how wonderfully Jesus replied to this request we see in the Lord's Prayer and in the two parables about prayer immediately following this question.

Have you ever said to Jesus, "Lord, teach me to pray"? He will answer you as He answered that unnamed disciple. He will teach *you* to pray. He will teach you through His Word, through the quiet leading of His Spirit, and through the circumstances of your life. But you must first of all ask Him to teach you.

OCTOBER 2

Now the Philistines fought against Israel and the men of Israel fled from before the Philistines, and fell down slain in mount Gilboa (1 SAMUEL 31:1).

Saul had lost the battle of life. His disobedience to God, his intrusion into the priest's office, his persecution of David, his unholy dealings with the witch of Endor—these were successive defeats in the fight everyone must make against sin. Now we come to the end. Over this last scene in the life of Israel's first king might well be written the New Testament word, "The wages of sin is death" (Romans 6:23).

Saul's tragic story shows us that nothing can take the place of obedience. As Samuel had said to him, "To obey is better than sacrifice" (1 Samuel 15:22). In the three thousand years since the time of Saul, God's demand for obedience has not changed. It is still required that we must obey God. We must obey Him in giving His Son priority in our lives. No sacrifice of time or money, no achievement in art or science, philanthropy or religion, can take the place of total obedience to the God who said of Jesus Christ, "This is my beloved Son, hear him" (Luke 9:35).

OCTOBER 3

A little yeast works through the whole batch of dough
(GALATIANS 5:9, NIV).

In this striking figure Paul shows that faith admits of no competing principle. Even as a tiny bit of yeast permeates a whole loaf, so only a little legalistic error, just a modicum of trusting to self-righteousness to win favor with God, can ruin the life of faith. God "saved us, not because of righteous things we have done but because of his mercy" (Titus 3:5, NIV). But the religion many are vainly trying to practice is a mixture of self-effort and dependence on God. The principle of faith underlies the spiritual life from beginning to end. So we need to take constant care that the yeast of legalism does not corrupt our walk with God.

OCTOBER 4

We love him, because he first loved us (1 JOHN 4:19).

There is an alternate reading of this beautiful sentence. According to high manuscript authority, it may read, "We love, because he first loved us." Far from diminishing the meaning of the verse, this reading broadens it to Christlike proportions. True, we love God because He first loved us. But the proof that we love God is our love for the brethren. That is exactly what the next verse tells us. For there John writes, "He that loveth not his brother whom he hath seen, how can he love God whom he hath not seen?" The love of God includes the love of our brethren; the love of our brethren includes the love of God. "But," someone asks, "do not all people love?" In the common human sense, yes; but in the deeper Christian sense, all people do not love. Christian love reflects the love of the Lord Jesus Christ; Christian love is willing to lay down its life for its friends. That kind of love is not natural to us; it comes from God who so loved us that He gave His only Son for our redemption.

OCTOBER 5

God, who at sundry times and in divers manners spake in time past unto the fathers by the prophets, hath in these last days spoken unto us by his Son (HEBREWS 1:1, 2a).

The majestic sentence that opens the epistle to the Hebrews begins with this assertion of the finality of Jesus Christ. To be sure, God has spoken in past ages. But His ultimate revelation is in His Son. Christ is the culmination. He is God's Word to the world. And according to this great declaration, He is also God's Word to us. Daily He speaks to us Christians through the Scriptures, through the witness of His Spirit within our hearts, and through the circumstances of our lives. Yes, God is speaking in Christ. Are we hearing what He says?

OCTOBER 6

And Aaron shall bear the names of the children of Israel in the breastplate of judgment upon his heart, when he goeth in unto the holy place, for a memorial before the Lord continually (EXODUS 28:29).

Here Aaron stands as a beautiful picture of the present work of the Lord Jesus Christ in behalf of all who belong to Him. As the first part of this chapter states, Aaron, the High Priest, wore over his heart a breastplate, magnificently woven in gold, blue, purple, and scarlet. In it were set four rows of precious stones, three stones in a row. On these stones—sardius, topaz, emerald, diamond, and other precious gems—were engraved the names of the twelve tribes of Israel. Therefore, when Aaron went into the holy place in the tabernacle, he was bearing, as it were, the names of God's people on his heart.

What a glorious portrayal of the work of Christ, our great High Priest, who ever lives to make intercession for us! Notice that Aaron went "in unto the holy place, for a memorial before the Lord continually." So the Lord Jesus Christ, bearing upon His heart the names of all His redeemed children, is continually in the Presence of the Father. The moment a Christian sins, either knowingly or unknowingly, Christ is before the throne of grace interceding for him. For as John tells us, "If anybody does sin, we have one who speaks to the Father in our defense—Jesus Christ, the Righteous One" (John 2:1, NIV).

OCTOBER 7

Therefore Eli said unto Samuel, Go, lie down: and it shall be, if he call thee, that thou shalt say, Speak, Lord; for thy servant heareth. So Samuel went and lay down in his place (1 SAMUEL 3:9).

"Speak, Lord; for thy servant heareth." Just suppose that young Samuel had not said that. Think what would have happened had this boy been unconcerned about obeying the voice of God. Israel might have lost Samuel's great career. God's people would have been the poorer without the ministry of this priest, prophet, and last of the judges. When a child responds to the call of God, great issues are in the making. Who can measure what it may mean for some boy and girl in Sunday school, to say nothing of your own child, to give his life to the Lord. No work for God has wider potentialities for good than Christian education, whether in school or in that crucial center of education—the home.

OCTOBER 8

By faith they passed through the Red Sea as by dry land: which the Egyptians assaying to do were drowned (HEBREWS 11:29).

Two multitudes—one, a military host, armed to the teeth and accompanied by horses and chariots of war; the other, a vast stream of humanity, women and children, young men and old men, unarmed and with no chariots and horses. But they both had to cross the Red Sea. All the world knows what happened. The Israelites passed through dry shod, but the waters engulfed the armies of Egypt. One multitude was armed with weapons; the other with faith. So there come for all of us times of peril when the waters of trial threaten to overwhelm us. Woe to them who entrust their safety to human resources alone; they will be swallowed up by the billows of trouble. But those who are armed with faith will pass through the deep waters in the safety of God's own care.

OCTOBER 9

But be sure to remember me when things go well with you. . . . the chief butler did not remember Joseph: he forgot him (GENESIS 40:14, 23, JB).

In reading this chapter we can hardly help becoming indignant at the negligence of the chief butler. Here is a man for whom Joseph had performed a great service. Yet despite Joseph's request that he be remembered, the chief butler, when he was restored to Pharaoh's favor, forgot him. "Surely," we say to ourselves, "that man was an ingrate. He should have told Pharaoh about Joseph at once. How could he forget the man who had been such a comfort in his imprisonment?"

How like that chief butler we are! Our Lord Jesus has commanded us to remember Him. And we do remember Him, particularly in our times of distress. But prosperity comes, all is well, and too often we forget Him to whom we owe our very soul's salvation. A test of Christian devotion is the extent to which, in happiness as well as in sorrow, we think of Jesus. How many times did your thoughts turn to Him yesterday?

OCTOBER 10

Peter therefore was kept in prison, but prayer was made without ceasing by the church unto God for him (ACTS 12:5).

We do not know exactly when Herod cast Peter into prison, nor do we know how long Peter remained there. It must, however, have been an imprisonment of some little duration because we read that he "was kept in prison" and that the church prayed "without ceasing." And when Peter was so wonderfully liberated, he returned to a prayer meeting (v. 12).

What a striking illustration of the title, Acts, of the book in which this incident is related! Here was a church with its leader in grave peril. Action was taken, not by appealing to Herod, not by planning a "prison-break" for Peter, but by praying. This is not to say that prayer is a substitute for other forms of Christian action so clearly enjoined in Scripture. Rather does it remind us of the necessity for prayer in every situation and show us that in itself prayer is vital Christian action.

OCTOBER 11

And the disciples did as Jesus directed them (MATTHEW 26:19, NEB).

While these words refer to the disciples' preparation of the Last Supper, they also have a broader meaning. There can be no finer comment on any Christian's life than the words: "he did as Jesus directed him." To Peter, James, John, and the others, Jesus spoke audibly. They heard His voice and many times, as in the case referred to in the text, did exactly what He told them to do. While He does not speak to us precisely as He did to the disciples, He nevertheless directs us. Through the Bible, in prayer and meditation, through some preacher or friend, or in the circumstances of life, we hear His voice. Of this we may be assured, Jesus does not leave us without directions for His service. Therefore if we do not do them, it is never His fault in failing to instruct us. Our part is always to keep a receptive mind, so that when He speaks we may hear Him and do as He directs us.

OCTOBER 12

One witness shall not rise up against a man for any iniquity, or for any sin, in any sin that he sinneth: at the mouth of two witnesses, or at the mouth of three witnesses, shall the matter be established (DEUTERONOMY 19:15).

In His great discourse in which He declared Himself the Light of the world, our Lord pointed to this verse. The Pharisees were objecting to His exalted claim to be "the light of the world" (John 8:12). In the course of His answer to their objection, He referred to this place in Deuteronomy, as He went on to say, "It is also written in your law, that the testimony of two men is true." Then he boldly declared, "I am one that beareth witness of myself, and the Father that sent me beareth witness of me" (John 8:17,18). What a clear assertion of the uniqueness of His ministry! Unlike many today who do not know their identity, the Lord Jesus Christ knew exactly why He was in the world and who He was. He knew that He was in a peculiar and special relationship to His heavenly Father. Yes, His self-witness is true, as millions of believing hearts on earth and the host of the redeemed in heaven know. Do you know it through the faith of your heart? Is Christ "the Light of the world" for you?

OCTOBER 13

*The slothful man saith, There is a lion without, I shall be
slain in the streets* (PROVERBS 22:13).

The Bible is not without humor and, all things considered,
Proverbs contains more wit than other parts of Scripture. Our
verse for today is evidence of this. With what subtle humor
Solomon describes the slothful man, as he sets down one of the
wild excuses to which laziness is prone! Determined to stay in
and take his ease, the slothful man fabricates the story that a
lion is loose in the street.

It is not without reason that Solomon makes laziness the tar-
get of his wit. While other sins ruin the testimony of believers,
common laziness also stultifies that of many of God's people.
How do we conquer laziness in the Christian life? How else
than by loving our Lord so much that we cannot be happy unless we are serving Him?

OCTOBER 14

And in mercy shall the throne be established (ISAIAH
16:5a).

Ever since men have ruled their fellowmen, governments have
been depending on force. And all along, thrones have toppled
and human might has failed. Authority founded upon force is
in the end bound to fall. But the Messianic throne of which
Isaiah is speaking is different. It is to be established in mercy;
it will have lasting dominion, because it is grounded in love.

If reliance upon force to bolster human government was costly
in the past, it is vastly more so today. Our world is at the brink
of a precipice because men have tapped destructive power of
such proportions as to threaten their own extinction. There is
only one power great enough to curb the forces of chaos, and
that is the power of the Gospel of Christ. Only the Gospel is
capable of changing hate to love, fear to trust, pride to humility,
and malice to mercy. And, regardless of human failure, the
throne of the Lord *will* be established in mercy. The kingdom is
coming. The reign of peace and righteousness for which this lost
and suffering world longs is no will-o'-the-wisp. Isaiah joins with
the other prophets in pointing us to a throne and kingdom that
are coming as surely as Christ our King will one day return.

OCTOBER 15

Let all bitterness, and wrath, and anger, and clamour, and evil speaking, be put away from you, with all malice (EPHESIANS 4:31).

That little word, "all," if we really heed it, is a sharp goad to our consciences. It does not discriminate between different forms of bitterness, wrath, and the like. Nor does it say that evil speaking is ever permissible. Instead it plainly says that *all* of these things must be put away from Christians. So look into your heart today and see whether you are cherishing some small bitterness, or just a little anger. See if you have been guilty of harboring a bit of malice or whether you have indulged in a few sentences of evil-speaking. Then recall that all these things are forbidden, and ask God through Christ to forgive you and help you put them entirely out of your life.

OCTOBER 16

Jesus knowing that the Father had given all things into his hands, and that he was come from God, and went to God; he riseth from supper (JOHN 13:3, 4a).

"Jesus knowing. . . ." When our Lord rose from supper and prepared Himself to wash the feet of the disciples, He did this knowing His divine origin, saving work, and heavenly destiny. Out of that knowledge of His unique relationship with the Father came this act of matchless condescension.

What prevents us from following our Lord's example of humble service? Well, for one thing, a false sense of dignity prevents us. Many a failure in Christian service comes from concern for our position before man, yes, even in the Church. If the Lord of glory, fully aware of His Deity, did not consider it beneath Him to take the place of a servant before His disciples, why should we allow our infinitely inferior position to prevent us from rendering any necessary service to others? Nothing is beneath a Christian, so long as it helps others and has in it no hint of moral compromise.

OCTOBER 17

Exceeding great and precious promises (2 PETER 1:4a).

Do you know the promises of God? Unfamiliarity with them weakens the prayer life. From Genesis to Revelation the Bible is full of promises from our heavenly Father, and every one of them is guaranteed by His integrity. You may be absolutely certain that somewhere in Scripture there is a promise from God precisely fitted to your need. To be definite in prayer honors the Heavenly Father. One of the assured avenues for prevailing prayer is to go before the Lord with some specific promise from His Word, to apply that promise in accord with its meaning, and then just to trust God to do for you as He wills.

OCTOBER 18

But he turned and said to Peter, "Get thee behind me, Satan; you are a hinderance to me, because your thoughts are not God's thoughts but men's" (MATTHEW 16:23, Weymouth).

This incident follows the account of Peter's great confession of Christ. With the best of human intentions but with complete lack of comprehension of the meaning of our Lord's declaration regarding His coming crucifixion (v. 21), Peter has dared remonstrate with Him. And now He who had blessed Peter for affirming His Deity calls His Apostle "Satan."

Why? Why should this very natural solicitude be so fiercely rebuked? The answer comes from the lips of Christ: "You are a hindrance to me, because your thoughts are not God's thoughts but men's." By that token, how often you and I, O Christian, are a hindrance to our Lord! Yes, we mean to serve Him and honestly try to do so. But our own thoughts get in the way. So the Lord Jesus through this rebuke of Peter teaches us that, in serving Him, mere human thoughts are not only inadequate, they can also be a hazard. We need His direction of our thoughts. The only mind sufficient to cope with spiritual issues is the mind of Christ. We who know Him by faith do have access to His mind; as Paul said to the Christians in Corinth, "We have the mind of Christ" (1 Corinthians 3:16). We have the Scriptures of truth; we are indwelt by the Spirit of Christ Ours, then, is the responsibility of being so committed to abide in Him and his Word that our thinking will be compatible with His

OCTOBER 19

Og the king of Bashan came out against us, he and all his people, to battle at Edrei. And the Lord said unto me, Fear him not: for I will deliver him, and all his people, and his land, into thy hand (DEUTERONOMY 3:1, 2).

Og king of Bashan was apparently the Goliath of the wilderness days. Verse eleven of this chapter speaks of him as a giant who had an iron bedstead no less than thirteen and one-half feet long and six feet broad. A formidable foe for Israel! But Moses and the people faced him in faith, trusting in the Lord's promise of deliverance.

Though no physical giants face us today, there is not a Christian who is not attacked from time to time by foes more formidable than Og king of Bashan. John Bunyan in *Pilgrim's Progress* describes how "Giant Despair" intimidated the pilgrims. How that giant can tower over us Christians, threatening our peace of mind! And he is only one of many a foe. What, then, are we to do when Giant Despair, and others like him, threaten us? Simply this: We are to remember that the same Lord who delivered Moses and Israel from Og king of Bashan will deliver us. We are to remember that the Lord whom we love and serve is able to deliver us from all our enemies, "for he who is in . . . [us] is greater than he who is in the world" (1 John 4:4, RSV).

OCTOBER 20

He then lying on Jesus' breast saith unto him, Lord, who is it? (JOHN 13:25).

As we read John's account of the Last Supper, we may feel almost envious of the beloved disciple's intimacy with the Lord Jesus. What nearness to Jesus this verse shows, as it describes John's leaning on His bosom! If this is our feeling, we may do well to remind ourselves that there is a sense in which John's intimacy with the Lord was not unique; for it is within the realm of possibility for any Christian who will truly draw near to the Lord Jesus in faith to be spiritually as close to the Saviour as the beloved disciple. Jesus has no favorites. His heart is big enough for all who love Him deeply. The nearer we draw to our Lord and the closer our walk with Him, the more assurance we shall feel of His love for us.

OCTOBER 21

The Lord is my portion, saith my soul; therefore will I hope in him (LAMENTATIONS 3:24).

It is a good thing for a child of God, whether Hebrew prophet or modern believer, to assert that the Lord is his portion. When Jeremiah wrote these words, his outward circumstances were tragic. But though he and his people had lost everything, nevertheless his soul reminded him that he still had the Lord. The day when we realize that the Lord really *is* our portion is a great one in our spiritual development. When that fact comes home to us, then we can affirm with Jeremiah, "Therefore will I hope in him."

OCTOBER 22

And he said, Let me go, for the day breaketh. And he said, I will not let thee go, except thou bless me (GENESIS 32:26).

The good in Jacob's character came to the fore in this memorable struggle he had with the angel of the Lord at the ford Jabbok. Realizing that it was no ordinary stranger who had accosted him, Jacob kept on wrestling. Surely the key to the higher side of this patriarch's character is contained in these words: "I will not let thee go, except thou bless me." Jacob became spiritually great, because the tenacity and persistence that were so much a part of him were being turned into spiritual channels. Throughout his life there runs this thread of eager reaching out for higher things and greater blessings.

We Christians may learn from the man who wrestled with the angel and would not let him go; we may learn that there is positively no substitute for perseverance in the spiritual life. Flashes of inspiration may come, but they can never take the place of the day-by-day walk with God. Our commonest spiritual failure goes back to the sin of not going daily, whatever happens, to the throne of grace and to our unwillingness to stay there long enough to receive the needed blessing. Would that we might be more like Jacob, who simply would not let go till he had the promised blessing!

OCTOBER 23

Abraham my friend (ISAIAH 41:8b).

What an honor! God actually called Abraham His friend. Truly this is a unique distinction, for the patriarch is the only man in the Old Testament thus honored.

But unique though this distinction is, the New Testament assures us that it may apply also to us. For the word "friend" leads on to the heart of the Gospel of John, where we read (John 15:14), "Ye are my friends, if ye do whatsoever I command you." Think of it! The title of honor given to Abraham alone may be yours and mine. There is but one qualification—to do what the Lord tells us. His will must be ours. When it comes to friendship with God, obedience is the password introducing us into a relationship of highest privilege. Are we really Christ's friends? Every one of us should be, for not one of us has ever been excused from doing what He asks us.

OCTOBER 24

The fear of the Lord is to hate evil (PROVERBS 8:13a).

The more famous statement about the fear, or reverent awe, of the Lord tells us that it is "the beginning of wisdom" (Proverbs 9:10). But while the fear of the Lord is indeed the beginning of wisdom, it must also tend to action—namely, the positive hatred of evil. The same thought, differently expressed, is stated in these words from the Nineteenth Psalm: "The fear of the Lord is clean, enduring for ever." What searching words! Think of them in this way. There can be no worship without the fear of the Lord in our hearts. But how far we fall short! When we come right down to it, do we really hate evil? "The fear of the Lord is clean." How easy it is to cling to just a little bit of evil, to treasure some sin, to cherish secretly a remnant of iniquity! But the divine word allows no exceptions. Let us be very slow to talk about being God-fearing, unless we are resolutely opposed to all evil.

OCTOBER 25

Is anything too hard for the Lord? (GENESIS 18:14a).

When the Lord asked Abraham that question, in his heart Abraham knew the answer. And we who follow in his footsteps of faith also know that nothing is too hard for the Lord. Yes, nothing that can ever happen to us is beyond His power to deal with perfectly. Every Christian knows that. He needs no elaborate theology to be assured of it. His heart tells him through the witness of the Spirit of God that nothing is too hard for the Lord in whom he trusts.

The next time you are in trouble and difficulties threaten to overwhelm you, stop fretting and take time simply to ask the question: "Is anything too hard for the Lord?" And as you answer it in faith that is willing to obey God and accept His will, He will give you His peace.

OCTOBER 26

Let every thing that hath breath praise the Lord. Praise ye the Lord (PSALM 150:6).

This Book of Psalms, the prayer book and hymnal of all God's people, closes in an unbroken paean of praise, sounded out by the last five psalms, which are really doxologies. Reading them is like looking back over the whole vast spiritual territory traversed in these matchless songs of the heart. These hundred fifty psalms run the gamut of spiritual experience. Joy and sorrow, confession and worship, remorse and anger, love and pity, all the motives of which the human heart is capable, are here reflected. Looking back over it all, the writer sees God as completely praiseworthy. No wonder the book ends with this universal call to praise: "Let every thing that hath breath praise the Lord." "Everything that hath breath." Who are we to say that, in their own inscrutable way, quite beyond human comprehension, even the animals may not be praising Him? "Praise ye the Lord." Yes, let us do it today; with all that is within us let us bless His holy Name.

OCTOBER 27

Wherefore, my beloved brethren, let every man be swift to hear, slow to speak, slow to wrath (JAMES 1:19).

No book in the New Testament is more like Proverbs than James, for none contains a greater concentration of practical wisdom. Addressed originally to the Jewish believers of the dispersion, its maxims are yet for every believer. We Christians need the book of James with its penetrating emphasis upon spiritual reality.

Consider this verse. First of all, we are to be alert to hear. Because God speaks in the silences of our lives, even the physically deaf may hear Him. Then, having heard the voice of God, we are to be slow to speak. For of all the varieties of folly, surely hasty speech is one of the most prevalent. A Christ-controlled tongue signifies a Christ-controlled heart. Such a heart, quick to hear the divine Word of truth, is always slow to speak an irresponsible or angry word.

OCTOBER 28

If we have forgotten the Name of our God, or stretched out our hands to a strange god, shall not God search this out? for he knoweth the secrets of the heart (PSALM 44:20, 21).

Very vividly the psalmist is reminding us that nobody departs from God with impunity. God knows all about those times when we forget Him. He knows when the thoughts of our hearts have gone out in worship to the strange gods of unholy desire, swollen pride, or obstinate self-will. Each of us, no matter how close to God at this present moment, should remember that there is no possibility of our deviating from fellowship with the Lord without His knowing it. Let all others think us pious and holy and good; God knows the secrets of our hearts. To realize this should bring us to Christ. Daily we stand in need of His control of our wayward thoughts and of His direction of our straying feet.

OCTOBER 29

Love the Lord thy God, and keep . . . his commandments.
. . . Love the Lord your God, and . . . serve him. . . . Love
the Lord your God, to walk in all his ways, and to cleave
unto him (DEUTERONOMY 11:1,13,22).

· Have you ever thought of the inseparable companions of
loving God? Here they are in these verses. Look at the sequence: love and keep, love and serve, love and walk, love and
cleave.

Do you love the Lord your God? Then you will be doing at
least four things in relation to Him. You will be keeping His
commandments (v. 1); you will be serving Him with all your
heart and with all your soul (v. 13); you will be walking in all
His ways (v. 22); and, finally, you will, whatever happens to
you, be holding fast to Him (v. 22).

Keep, serve, walk, and cleave. Are these the companions of
the love of God we profess in prayer and sing about in church?
Without His love "poured out . . . into our hearts by the Holy
Spirit" (Romans 5:5, NIV), we are indeed as "sounding brass
or a tinkling cymbal," while without doing these four things
our protestation of love for the Lord our God is devoid of reality.

OCTOBER 30

Forty and two years old was Ahaziah when he began to
reign. . . . His mother's name . . . was Athaliah. . . . He also
walked in the ways of the house of Ahab: for his mother
was his counsellor to do wickedly (2 CHRONICLES 22:2, 3).

These verses stress parental responsibility. Contrary to pres-
ent-day sentimentality, the fact that a woman is a mother does
not in itself make her good. There are many noble mothers. And
there are also some mothers who, like Athaliah, lead their
children in the way of destruction. But a mother does not have
to be an Athaliah nor a father an Ahab to lead a child astray.
Inconsistency of example, placing social or business obligations
before duty to children, lack of love—such things may cause
even a Christian parent to be a stumbling block to a child. As
someone has said, "What you do speaks so loudly that I can't
hear what you say." There is no more basic responsibility than
Christian parenthood, and it takes much prayer and an abund-
ance of faith and love to bring up a child in the way he should
go.

OCTOBER 31

Wilt thou show wonders to the dead? shall the dead arise and praise thee? Selah. Shall thy loving kindness be declared in the grave? or thy faithfulness in destruction? Shall thy wonders be known in the dark? and thy righteousness in the land of forgetfulness? (PSALM 88:10,11, 12).

No psalm exceeds this one in its midnight hues. With sombre beauty it sounds the depths. Beginning with a lament, it ends in darkness, and in its center are these six questions. Look at them carefully, for they have something to say to us.

The afflicted saint who first penned these questions undoubtedly thought of their answers as negative. Living as he did before the full manifestation of God's grace in Christ's atonement and resurrection, there was for him little light beyond the grave. In his affliction of soul he felt that death ended all.

But you and I who are blest with a knowledge of the Gospel know that for every one of these six questions we have a positive reply. The New Testament assures us that God will show wonders to the dead and that they will arise and praise Him. It tells us that through the risen Christ loving-kindness is declared in the grave; that His faithfulness does transcend destruction; that wonders are known in the dark and His righteousness in the land of forgetfulness.

Here, then, is a passage to remember when sorrow and depression cloud our skies. Truly we are highly favored in comparison with the suffering Israelite who wrote this beautiful complaint. The Christian life would be a shallow experience were it all sunlight. Dark valleys must be traversed on the way to the heavenly city. But by God's grace we know the Light of the world who shines in the darkness and who can never be overpowered by it.

NOVEMBER 1

It is the Lord Christ you are serving (Colossians 3:24, NIV).

What a privilege for us Christians! We are in the personal service of the King of kings and Lord of lords. It is an honor to work in close relationship with some great man or woman. But what is that to the high privilege of being in the service of the Lord Jesus Christ? Really to serve Him is no mere formality; it is a very personal thing—so personal as to be a matter of daily and hourly companionship. In a practical sense our service for Christ is what we make it. He wants it to be a fruitful experience for us. On His part He would give abundant blessings to those who serve Him. But it is we who restrict these blessings by keeping at a distance from Him. So may this month be for us a time of closer fellowship with the Lord Christ whom we are serving.

NOVEMBER 2

For we have not an high priest which cannot be touched with the feeling of our infirmities; but was in all points tempted like as we are, yet without sin (Hebrews 4:15).

Today we think about a beautiful phrase from a well-loved verse—"touched with the feeling of our infirmities." The context speaks of Christ our High Priest, and how He understands our human condition. The Greek verb translated "touched with the feeling of" is *sympathesai,* meaning "suffer with," and it lies behind our English word "sympathize." As for "infirmities," they should not be understood as applying only to our physical weaknesses. The wonderful truth is that our Lord sympathizes with all our infirmities, whether physical, mental, or spiritual.

For sheer comfort few truths can compare with this fact of the sympathizing Christ. He knows what we suffer, because He Himself lived this life on earth and was one with our humanity. He met the same trials and temptations we meet and was victorious over them all. He understands all about us and out of His loving sympathy is interceding for us before the throne of grace.

NOVEMBER 3

Walk worthy of God (I Thessalonians 2:12).

Have you ever heard the appeal, "Don't do it; it's not worthy of you"? It is a valid one, and with those who have a decent self-image it is often effective. But it is weak indeed, compared with the scriptural appeal for us to "walk worthy of God." That is a truly exalted plea! Many things we might consider worthy of us as secular beings are quite incompatible with really walking with God. Let us make that criterion our own today so that we may be worthy of Christ, who is our Immanuel, our God with us.

NOVEMBER 4

For look how high the heaven is in comparison of the earth;
so great is his mercy also toward them that fear him.
Look how wide also the east is from the west; so far hath
he set our sins from us (Psalm 103:11, 12, Book of Common Prayer).

The merit of this old translation, antedating the King James Version, lies in its use of the word "look."

Said Goethe, "If the rainbow stood for a day, no one would look at it." The heavens are ever over us, high above the earth. But like the ever present mercies of God, they are so familiar that we seldom pause to look at them. Similarly, God's forgiveness of our sins may be taken for granted like the distance between east and west, so familiar and yet so mysterious. Yet when we pause to reflect upon the wonders of the heavens and their height above the earth; when we take time to think about the marvels of space—above all, when we apply these beautiful words of the psalmist to God's mercy to us, then we can only bow in wonder and adoration before Him. It is a good thing to take a long look at all God has done for us sinners.

NOVEMBER 5

And be ye kind one to another, tenderhearted, forgiving one another, even as God for Christ's sake hath forgiven you (EPHESIANS 4:32).

Here Paul describes our attitude in relation to other people by saying, "Be ye kind one to another." "Why," some one remarks, "that's elementary." Yes, it is elementary, but no advancement in devotion and religious knowledge will ever supersede it. For the lack of simple kindness in human relations can ruin the witness of an otherwise zealous and dedicated believer. The true Christian life has no place for hard-hearted disciples. No one who has ever experienced the grace of Christ in the forgiveness of sins should ever be ungracious to other people. Being kind to others for our Lord's sake shows the world who we are.

NOVEMBER 6

For Herod feared John . . . and heard him gladly. . . . and when the daughter of the said Herodias came in, and danced, and pleased Herod . . . the king said . Ask of me whatsoever thou wilt, and I will give it thee . . and . . . the king . . . commanded his head to be brought (MARK 6:20, 22, 27).

This is the condensed record of a great tragedy Notice the successive steps as you read the complete story (Mark 6:14-29). John the Baptist had denounced Herod's unlawful marriage to Herodias, his brother's wife, yet Herod feared and gladly heard the Lord's messenger. Up to that point there was hope for the king. But then he made a promise to Herodias. That promise nullified his response to John, and led to murdering him who was the very voice of God.

How clearly this shows the peril of compromise! God's messages come to us in different ways—through Scripture, through worship, through circumstances, or through friends. Like Herod we hear them gladly. But we may make a liaison with some evil thing. We may be bound to an unworthy habit. A selfish indulgence may claim our allegiance. And finally, when the choice has to be made, we may disregard God's message and continue in wrongdoing. But it does not have to be that way; unlike Herod we may obey the voice of God and, putting away compromising things in our lives, repent.

NOVEMBER 7

Behold, the eye of the Lord is upon them that fear him, upon them that hope in his mercy (PSALM 33:18).

"The eye of the Lord." There you have one of the most awe-inspiring phrases in Scripture. The thought of divine omniscience, the gaze that penetrates into all of life, is enough to strike with fear those who acknowledge God's existence but do not know His forgiveness and His love. For us Christians, however, the thought of God's all-seeing eye brings reassurance. We know that the eye of the Almighty is upon us for good; we know that His gaze is a tender one, watchful with the eye of a loving Heavenly Father. And therefore we shrink from anything that would displease the Lord who did so much for us. One thing is certain of all our acts and our thoughts also. The eye of the Lord sees them. What an incentive to the holiness of life to which we are called (1 Peter 1:15, 16)!

NOVEMBER 8

And as he [Paul] reasoned of righteousness, temperance [self-control], and judgment to come, Felix trembled, and answered, Go thy way for this time; when I have a convenient season, I will call for thee (ACTS 24:25).

Was there ever anyone who had a better chance than Felix? God made it possible for him to hear the truth from the lips of the greatest missionary who ever lived. It was no superficial message Paul gave Felix but one powerful enough to make him tremble. And then Felix imperiled his soul—not by persecuting Paul, not by denouncing him, not by blaspheming the truth he taught, but simply by putting him off. So Felix stands as a monument to the dangerous error of deferring one's response to God until another time.

If God's Spirit, whether through a witness like Paul, through the Bible, or in any other way, is striving with a person, that person puts off his response at his soul's peril. To be sure, he may seek to find a more "convenient season," but it may turn out more convenient for the devil than for God. Nor does this apply only to unbelievers. God also reasons with us Christians about "righteousness, temperance [self-control], and judgment to come," and when He does we had better respond to what He says.

NOVEMBER 9

Exercise thyself rather unto godliness (1 Timothy 4:7).

Here Paul uses the Greek word *gymnazein* (from which we get "gymnasium") for the exercise of the inner man. And when it comes to persistence in exercising, is it not true that the dedicated athlete puts many Christians to shame? Think of the rigors of self-discipline, the hard training men and women persevere in for the sake of sports. Then compare the meager efforts many believers—and some Christian workers also—are making for their spiritual development. No wonder so many Christians are spiritually flabby.

Just imagine the good things that would happen if young Christians—and older ones too—would really go into training through the daily discipline of prayer and Scripture meditation. To keep in condition for serving the Lord requires unremitting faithfulness. What about your spiritual fitness?

NOVEMBER 10

God has made this Jesus, whom you crucified, both Lord and Christ (Acts 2:36, NEB).

"But," you say, "Peter was speaking to the Jews who had crucified Christ. What wicked people they were for killing their own Messiah!" But pause a moment, Christian friend. You too have your share in that crime of the ages. You cannot be a Christian without acknowledging that your Lord died on Calvary not only because of the Jews, or because of Pilate's weakness, but also because of you. Through your sin you too are implicated in nailing the Son of God to the cross, and it was to atone for your transgressions that He hung and suffered there.

So Peter was also referring to you and me when he said, "God has made this Jesus, whom you crucified, both Lord and Christ."

Yes, God has made him both Lord and Christ. Well, what have we made Him? We call Him our Saviour from sin, but is He also our Lord, the sovereign of everything we have and are?

NOVEMBER 11

And Ruth the Moabitess said unto Naomi, Let me now go to the field, and glean ears of corn after him in whose sight I shall find grace (RUTH 2:2).

Here Ruth uses the word "grace." And her experience is indeed one of the great Old Testament illustrations of this great word. For in this beautiful little book, she is frequently referred to as "Ruth the Moabitess" (1:22, 2:21). Surely the author wants to impress upon the reader the fact of her nationality. Why? Well, turn to Deuteronomy 23:3 and read the sweeping prohibition against the entrance of a Moabite into the congregation of the Lord down to the tenth generation. Ruth belonged to that proscribed people; one of the heathen Gentiles, she was an alien with no claim upon the blessings promised God's chosen people. But she was blessed in spite of her origin. Even more, she was singled out to be one of the few women whose names are included in the genealogy of our Lord Jesus Christ (Matthew 1:5). Such is God's grace—wider than any national barriers; greater by far than any human merit.

NOVEMBER 12

And when he was in affliction, he besought the Lord his God, and humbled himself greatly before the God of his fathers (2 CHRONICLES 33:12).

It is strange that a king of such exemplary life as Hezekiah had a son of such excessive wickedness as Manasseh. In the first part of his long reign of fifty-five years, Manasseh deliberrately cultivated evil. He seems to have made the most determined efforts to undo all the good his father had accomplished. Then something happened. Manasseh ran afoul of the King of Assyria and was taken captive. Coming to his senses, he sought the Lord in humility and repentance. Nevertheless, so great had been his wickedness that one hardly escapes a sense of shock in reading that God spared him (v. 13).

F. B. Meyer once said, "There is hope for any sinner if Manasseh could be saved." While that is true, we must not presume on this unusual example of God's grace. We need to remember the many other sinners like Jeroboam and Ahab, Jezebel and Athaliah, who continued in wickedness and never repented. To linger in sin is to imperil one's soul. Today, not tomorrow, is the time for repentance.

NOVEMBER 13

When God was about to send his first-born into the world, he also said, "All of God's angels must worship him" (HEBREWS 1:6, TEV).

We have only to face the implications of this declaration to see the obligation of worshiping Christ. For if God commanded all the angels to worship His Son, we also, who are "made a little lower than the angels" (Psalm 8:5), must adore Him.

There are many things in life we deem necessary, but of these only a few are essential. And among these essential things is the worship of Christ. Lacking it, our days are incomplete with an incompleteness that disregards the exalted place God has given His Son. Let us bow today in thankful adoration and glad worship before Him, whom the Father has so highly honored.

NOVEMBER 14

He who obeys his command remains in him and he in him (1 JOHN 3:24, Berkeley).

Nothing in the Christian life is more basic than abiding in Christ; few things are more misunderstood. But with the clarity so characteristic of his writings the Apostle John here tells us how to abide in Christ. The way to do it is to keep on obeying Him. Keep Christ's commands and you remain in Him. That is what John is saying. It is significant that the verb translated "remains" is the same one employed by our Lord Himself when He said, "Abide in me and I in you" (John 15:4). So John is saying to us: "He who obeys his commands abides in him."

This illustrates the practicality of spiritual truth. Mysticism would link abiding in Christ with ecstatic experiences; John identified it with our plain, everyday obedience to the Lord, and so brings it within the range of us all. Obey your Lord and you will be abiding in Him. This is one of the first principles of Christian living.

NOVEMBER 15

Let everyone that nameth the name of Christ depart from iniquity (2 TIMOTHY 2:19b).

There is a good deal to the old saying that people are known by the company they keep. And no Christian has any right to companionship with evil. Our commitment to Jesus as Saviour and Lord means that there are some associates we must give up, some practices we must depart from. Every now and then we need to take stock and ask ourselves, "Have I departed from all known sin in my life? Have I made a clean break with iniquity? What kind of company am I keeping in my thoughts?" These are searching questions, and today may be a good time to face them.

NOVEMBER 16

For I know that my redeemer liveth (JOB 19:25).

What precious words! We sing them in our churches, we hear them preached from our pulpits, we marvel at them as a high point of revelation back in the dim past when Job lived. Is there anything new we may say about them? Perhaps not; but we may nevertheless find it helpful to emphasize two words. Said Job, "I *know!*" Here is the spectacle of a man long before this age of grace and without the Gospel knowledge that is ours, who said of the Redeemer, "I *know!*" How wonderful that Job did not exclaim, "I hope." No, he actually knew! And what was it he knew? "I know," he said, "that my redeemer *liveth.*"

It may be, as many say, that Job lived in primitive times, even before the giving of the law through Moses. If so, it only makes him the greater saint. So let us be thinking now about our growth in spiritual knowledge. Let us be asking ourselves whether we have gone as far as Job did long ago. Do we really, without any doubt or equivocation, know that our Redeemer lives? Is the object of all our worship and love the living Christ who died and rose again, the Redeemer who ascended into heaven and is coming back again?

NOVEMBER 17

*In my flesh shall I see God. Whom I shall see for myself,
and mine eyes shall behold, and not another* (JOB 19:26,
27).

Job continues the great affirmation we considered yesterday.
Now he voices his conviction that his future sight of God will
be a personal one. "Whom I shall see for myself," was his confident expectation in relation to God. But unlike him many of
us are content with a secondhand religious experience. We read
books by those who have walked closely with God, we sit under
preachers who speak directly regarding Him, and then continue to be satisfied with the second best. Yet all the time it is
possible for us, who have what Job did not have—the New
Testament revelation of Christ—it is possible for us to know
God for ourselves in a very personal way. "For God, who commanded the light to shine out of darkness, hath shined in our
hearts, to give the light of the knowledge of the glory of God
in the face of Jesus Christ" (2 Corinthians 4:6).

NOVEMBER 18

My heart trusted in him, and I am helped (PSALM 28:7).

The logic of cause and effect is no less active in the spiritual
than in the physical realm. God's dealings with men are orderly;
His ways are characterized by reliability, not by confusion. So
there are certain things that, when we do them, are followed
by sure results. Take, by way of illustration, our text for today.
"My heart," David said, "trusted in him." That is the cause.
David did a very simple but essential thing. He trusted God in
his heart. Therefore, he experienced the result expressed in the
brief words, "I am helped."

Such spiritual logic is irrefutable. God being God, we may
affirm that, when we really trust Him in our hearts, no other
result will follow but that of our being helped. Whether the
help is given us immediately or whether it comes later on is
secondary. The fact remains that the Lord does not fail to help
those who put their trust in Him.

NOVEMBER 19

He is before all things . . . that in all things he might have the preeminence (COLOSSIANS 1:17, 18).

This is Christ's eternal and rightful place. He who said of Himself, "Before Abraham was I am" (John 8:58) *is* before all things. To Him God has given the primacy in everything.

As for us, we are God's creatures—finite yet made in His image, fallen yet capable of redemption through Christ. God has given us the responsibility of spiritual and moral choice. And so it is possible for us to deny Christ the supremacy God desires Him to have in us. So there are actually those who are placing the preeminent Christ second to themselves and their own desires. Think of it! Relegating the divine Son of God to an inferior position in one's life!

"He is before all things." This is the place of primacy God has given His dear Son. Does He have it in you?

NOVEMBER 20

And it came to pass, when he had made an end of speaking unto Saul, that the soul of Jonathan was knit with the soul of David, and Jonathan loved him as his own soul. . . . Then Jonathan and David made a covenant, because he loved him as his own soul (1 SAMUEL 18:1, 3).

In the next verse, we read that Jonathan took his clothing and gave it to David, stripping off even his sword, bow, and belt. What an example of true friendship!

Was David ever ashamed of Jonathan? Certainly not. Why, he knew that, in the providence of God, he owed Jonathan his salvation from present harm. He realized that he could at any time trust Jonathan with his life. All Jonathan had, even his own garments and weapons, was David's.

Among human relationships, friendship occupies a unique place. And its annals contain no higher example than the love of Jonathan and David. David was in deep trouble when Saul's unbalanced mind turned against him. Yet God graciously gave him a friend. There are few greater joys than those of friendship in the Lord.

NOVEMBER 21

The Lord thy God in the midst of thee is mighty; he will save, he will rejoice over thee with joy; he will rest in his love, he will joy over thee with singing (ZEPHANIAH 3:17).

What beautiful things this verse contains! It shows us where the Lord God is—"in the midst of." His people. It describes Him in one great word, "mighty." It tells us what He does for His people—"saves." Then it lets us look into His loving heart, as it speaks of Him rejoicing, resting in His love, and joying over His people with singing. Though Zephaniah is a severe book of judgment, it closes with this lovely assurance of God's saving power and His love.

NOVEMBER 22

He asked them, "Who do the crowds say I am?" . . . "But what about you?" he asked, "Who do you say I am?" (LUKE 9:18, 20, NIV).

The most important issue before the world today is set forth in these two questions Jesus asked at Caesarea Philippi. The first ("Who do the crowds say I am?") the easier of the two, contrasts with the second. And the disciples were able to answer it, for verse nineteen tells us that they replied, "Some say John the Baptist; others say Elijah, and still others, that one of the prophets of long ago has come back to life" (NIV).

So they reported quite accurately the sentiments of others concerning the Lord Jesus. But when it came to our Lord Jesus' second question, "Who do you say I am?" there was a difference. The very disciples who had been living with him in intimate fellowship and who had seen His mighty works, were strangely silent. Then one of them, Peter, spoke up and gave the answer in his historic confession, "The Christ of God," or, as Matthew gives it more completely, "You are the Christ, the Son of the living God" (Matthew 16:16, NIV).

The significance of these questions and answers cannot be overestimated. It is not what others think of Christ that counts for us, but what we ourselves think of Him. Though the Lord does inquire into the beliefs of others, at the same time He is holding us responsible for our own estimate of Him. Our faith in Jesus Christ is either personal or it is nothing.

NOVEMBER 23

You also joining in helping us through your prayers . . .
(2 CORINTHIANS 1:11, NASB).

You may be unable to give liberally to the Lord's work. But, fellow believer, how much you can help, how much you really can give! Why, you can give your time in the greatest Christian work there is—intercessory prayer. Have you a prayer list? Do you regularly bring before the throne of grace your church, your pastor, your sick friends or neighbors, missionaries in far places, Christian workers in the cities of the nation? Are you "joining in helping" them through your prayers? Prayer is at the dynamic center of Christian service. Are you giving yourself to it?

NOVEMBER 24

Oh, that men would praise the Lord for his goodness, and for his wonderful works to the children of men!
(PSALM 107:8).

This refrain is repeated four times in this psalm. It is a reminder, not only from the heart of the psalmist who stands aside, as it were, looking at mankind, but also from God. Read through the whole psalm, and you will see some vivid illustrations of God's recurring mercies toward all men and especially toward the redeemed. The various stanzas marked off by the refrain tell the repeated tale of God's grace.

"Oh, that men would praise the Lord for his goodness, and for his wonderful works to the children of men!" Is it not sad that such a refrain has to be uttered? It would indeed be far better if we were so quick to praise the Lord that no reminder was necessary. But that is not the case. Men receive God's favors in good measure, pressed down and running over, yet few stop even to thank Him.

Let us not hesitate to admit that we also need this reminder; we too need it constantly, just as it appears in this psalm. So let us pause right now and praise the Lord for His goodness and for His wonderful works to us.

NOVEMBER 25

A new commandment I give unto you, That ye love one another; as I have loved you, that ye also love one another (JOHN 13:34).

No Christian will ever come to the place of not needing to remind himself constantly of this new commandment—a commandment so familiar that it is frequently overlooked. Just loving one another in the way He has loved us—that is the inescapable obligation our Lord lays upon us. It is His very own criterion for our discipleship. However much we may talk about the soundness of our doctrine, we must remember that obedience to Christ's new commandment is the essential validation of our discipleship. For He went on to say, "By this shall all men know that ye are my disciples, if ye have love one to another" (v. 35). No mutual love among Christians, no vital witness to the world—that is why the new commandment is so imperative.

NOVEMBER 26

I Tertius, who wrote this epistle, salute you in the Lord (ROMANS 16:22).

Here we see that God has a place in His work for everyone. Tertius knew shorthand, which was practiced in the Roman Empire of the first century. While not gifted as a preacher and teacher like Paul, he had his own talent and placed it at the Apostle's disposal.

Was ever secretary or stenographer more honored than Tertius? By reason of its influence in human life this epistle is acknowledged to be the greatest letter ever written. What a privilege to have been used as the amanuensis for such a letter! The Lord did not give Tertius an intellect capable of organizing and writing this greatest of the epistles. But what He did give him was an attentive ear and a skilled pen capable of accurately setting down Paul's inspired words. And who would say that Tertius's consecrated stenography was less pleasing to the Lord than Paul's consecrated genius? What about your talents? Are they fully at the Lord's disposal?

NOVEMBER 27

Howbeit there was no reckoning made with them of the money that was delivered into their hand, because they dealt faithfully (2 KINGS 22:7).

The reference is to the temple workmen—the carpenters, builders, and masons—at the time of Josiah. They were employed to repair the Lord's house. So great was their reputation for honesty that no formal reckoning was required; the word of these workmen was enough.

It is a mistake to speak of "common honesty." Honesty is all too uncommon. No virtue, least of all honesty, is a small thing. Let the remembrance of these ancient workmen of such great integrity remind us of the preciousness of honesty; and let us also remember that though we Christians are under grace, none of us is ever exempt from maintaining the highest standards of integrity in all we do.

NOVEMBER 28

And the Lord shut him in (GENESIS 7:16).

Noah was safe. He was safe not because of what he had done, but because God shut him in. It was God, not Noah, who saved the patriarch, his family, and the animals with them from the catastrophic judgment of the deluge.

"And the Lord shut him in." These six words speak of the finality of salvation through Christ. To His suffering on the cross for the sin of the world nothing can ever be added. The work of Calvary is a finished work. Not in the slightest is it dependent upon human effort. It is God Himself who, as Isaiah declared, made our Lord's "soul an offering for sin" (Isaiah 53:10). It is God alone who, as Paul said, "was in Christ, reconciling the world unto himself" (2 Corinthians 5:19). It is God who "so loved the world, that He gave His only begotten Son, that whosoever believeth in him should not perish, but have everlasting life" (John 3:16). It is God, as Paul further said, who "made him to be sin for us, who knew no sin" (2 Corinthians 5:21). The soul that leans on Jesus is as safe from present or future condemnation as Noah was from the flood.

NOVEMBER 29

I beseech you therefore, brethren, by the mercies of God, that ye present your bodies a living sacrifice, holy, acceptable unto God, which is your reasonable service (ROMANS 12:1).

This may well be the most eloquent appeal for consecration ever made. Notice the foundation upon which it rests. "I beseech you therefore," pleads Paul, "by the mercies of God." What are these "mercies of God?" They are nothing less than the great doctrines of grace, so powerfully and fully set forth in the preceding chapters of this epistle. That any Christian who knows these doctrines and is familiar with God's provision for justification and sanctification through His Son, should deliberately refuse to present his body a living sacrifice is indeed difficult to understand. The surest way to lead others into the blessedness of the surrendered life is to ground them in the doctrines of grace. When anyone really grasps the wonder of what Christ has done for him, then his surrender to his Lord follows as the ready response of a grateful heart.

NOVEMBER 30

In my distress I cried unto the Lord, and he heard me (PSALM 120:1).

Have you ever thought of distress as an indispensable accompaniment of spiritual living? Yet such it assuredly is. After all, we are so constituted that difficulty, not joy, draws us closest to our God. Shakespeare said, "Sweet are the uses of adversity," but did not make the full spiritual application. One of the older commentators who speaks of "the wondrous advantage of trouble" is more nearly right when he points out that this "advantage" lies in the fact that trouble leads us to call upon God. Not only so, but when we cry to Him in our distress, the result is that God hears us, because He is always attentive to the cries of His children.

Far from being mere theory, these things are the very warp and woof of Christian living. We have only to look into our lives to recognize their truth. All of us have firsthand knowledge of help arising out of distress. James wrote truly when he opened his epistle with this challenge: "Consider it pure joy, my brethren, whenever you face trials of many kinds" (James 1:2, NIV)

DECEMBER 1

The Son is the radiance of God's glory (HEBREWS 1·3, NIV).

Here is a truth about Christ that blazes with light. Our Lord, who for our sakes became poor and who humbled Himself through the death of the cross, is the effulgence of God's glory. All the vast heavens contain no star so bright as Christ. When the skies themselves will have vanished, Christ will continue to shine. In Him God has concentrated the splendor of His eternal Being. No wonder that during His earthly ministry the Lord Jesus said, "I am the light of the world" (John 8:12).

Are you reflecting His radiance? You may do so, for He, who is the brightness of God's glory, has condescended to live within us Christians, illuminating our lives so that we may manifest His radiance to those who walk in darkness. In His Sermon on the Mount Jesus said of us," You are the light of the world. . . . Let your light so shine before men, that they may see your good works and give glory to your Father who is in heaven" (Matthew 5:14, 16, RSV).

DECEMBER 2

Therefore, having these promises, beloved, let us cleanse ourselves from all defilement of flesh and spirit, perfecting holiness in the fear of God (2 CORINTHIANS 7:1, NASB).

Paul has just referred to some of the Old Testament promises of what God will do for His people when they separate themselves from evil. Now he urges us to cleanse ourselves from "all defilement of the flesh." That means carnality of life and walk. But such cleansing, though necessary, is not enough. One may be ascetically pure and yet be a very bad person. So the cleaning must also be "from all defilement . . . of spirit."

Some who stress "the separated life" are so concerned about certain worldly practices that they overlook the necessity for separation from spiritual defilement. Though their habits may be above reproach and though they indulge in no gross practices, religious people who are proud or unmerciful or unloving are far from clean before God. So Paul adds, "perfecting holiness in the fear of God," or as *Today's English Version* renders it, "let us seek to be completely holy, by living in the fear of God." It is a high aim and only the Spirit of Christ, who lives in our hearts by faith, can help us realize it.

DECEMBER 3

Being fruitful in every good work (COLOSSIANS 1:10).

While probably no Christian has ever reached greater heights of spiritual experience than Paul, none was more practical-minded. He knew that faith in the Lord Jesus must lead to a concern for others that finds expression in deeds of love and mercy.

Many of us pray and read our Bibles daily; we go to church and prayer meetings. But what about our fruitfulness for the Lord? The proof of the reality of our love for God lies in the extent of our productivity in every good work. As John said, "My children, love must not be a matter of words and talk; it must be genuine and show itself in action" (1 JOHN 3:18, NEB).

DECEMBER 4

And the goat shall bear upon him all their iniquities unto a land not inhabited: and he shall let go the goat in the wilderness (LEVITICUS 16:22).

The central day in Old Testament worship is described in this chapter. It was the tenth day of the seventh month (September-October) in the Hebrew calendar and is still known in Judaism as Yom Kippur, the Day of Atonement. Only on that day was the high priest—and he alone—permitted to go into the holy of holies. Having first sacrificed a bullock as a sin offering for himself, he then brought two goats before the Lord and cast lots over them. The goat on which the Lord's lot fell was sacrificed (v. 15) and its blood sprinkled on the mercy seat (the top of the ark of the covenant). This typified the blood of Christ covering the sinner's transgression and effecting his forgiveness and reconciliation with God.

The other goat, referred to in the verse for today, was the scapegoat. On its head the high priest laid his hands and confessed all the iniquities of Israel. Then the scapegoat was led out into the wilderness, where it was released. So another aspect of salvation—that of the remission of sins—was typified.

All this portrays what God has done for us in Christ. In Him we are reconciled and all our sins put away. To worry over sins that have been forgiven is not pleasing to God. What He does not remember, we should forget. Well may we say with David, "Blessed is he whose transgression is forgiven, whose sin is covered" (Psalm 32:1).

DECEMBER 5

He that hath no rule over his own spirit is like a city that is broken down, and without walls (PROVERBS 25:28).

It is surprising how easy it is to narrow down the Word of God. When Solomon speaks of a man ruling his spirit, most of us think of controlling our temper. Yet that is just one aspect of ruling our own spirit. Some of us who have mild tempers are yet plagued with moods. We must rule them, because it is just as wrong to give in to a mood of discouragement or apathy as it is to fly into a towering rage. In either case our spirit rules us, and we are not the master of the city that is our personality.

Solomon is right. Let your moods govern you, whether they be moods of anger, discouragement, or worry, and your defenses are down. Your personality is at the mercy of the enemy. That way lies ill health— physical and emotional. But you and I do not have to give in to ourselves, for one of the fruits of the Holy Spirit, who dwells in every Christian, is self-control (Galatians 5:22, 23, RSV). True self-mastery comes from Christ's control of our minds and emotions.

DECEMBER 6

These are the statutes and judgments, which ye shall observe to do in the land, which the Lord God of thy fathers giveth thee to possess it, all the days that ye live upon the earth (DEUTERONOMY 12:1).

Moses is stressing the necessity of obedience to God's commandments. And in doing so he defines the duration of Israel's obedience by the words, "all the days that ye live upon the earth."

Christians are not under the law of Moses; they are under the royal law of Christ. But spiritual principles do not change with different times. God still demands of His children continuous obedience. "All the days that you live upon the earth" applies to our obedience just as much as to that of the ancient Israelites. It is perilous to forget that God permits no parentheses in obeying Him. We cannot play at being Christians; we cannot choose to serve the Lord one day and ourselves another. If we are His, we are His forever, because He claims our full allegiance "all the days that [we] live upon the earth."

DECEMBER 7

Thus saith the Lord of hosts, the God of Israel, Amend your ways and your doings (JEREMIAH 7:3).

If ever a people belonging to God needed to be called back from folly and apostasy, it was Judah. But we miss something by confining ourselves just to the historical situation, important though it is. The Word of God speaks to all generations. It is still speaking to us today. "Amend your ways and your doings." Human nature and sin being what they are, each of us is called on to rectify his life in the sight of God. We who study the Bible need to stop and apply it to ourselves. Are we, as an outcome of our knowledge of holy things, living good lives? No detailed and specialized knowledge of Scripture can for a moment take the place of living a holy life to the glory of God. Yes, we too are called to "amend [our] ways and [our] doings."

DECEMBER 8

And the Lord appeared unto him in the plains of Mamre. . . . and, lo, three men stood by him (GENESIS 18:1, 2).

Here God comes to Abraham. As this remarkable chapter shows, He comes to him as a guest. (It is a theophany, a visible manifestation of God; for the chief of the three visitors was undoubtedly Jehovah Himself.)

Think of it! Abraham had the privilege of entertaining God. "But," some one says, "that was a privilege never to be repeated." Not so, for God has at other times and in other ways come to men. Think of the many who, when the Lord Jesus lived among men nineteen hundred years ago, had fellowship with Him. Think also of those two on the Emmaus road (Luke 24); they had the privilege of entertaining the risen Lord Jesus, though at first, like Abraham, they did not recognize their Guest. And the very center of the New Testament teaching about the relationship between Christ and the believer is that through the Holy Spirit the Lord Jesus Himself makes His home in our hearts by faith. If you are a Christian, then what Paul called "this mystery among the Gentiles; which is Christ in you, the hope of glory" (Colossians 1:27) applies to you. Is yours a life that is really making Him welcome?

DECEMBER 9

The Lamb slain from the foundation of the world (REVE-
LATION 13:8).

A writer of religious books once called the cross an after-
thought with God. But he was wrong. God has no afterthoughts.
He knows the end from the beginning. Though it is true that
the cross came at a particular point in human history, it is
also true that the Lamb was "slain from the foundation of the
world" (Revelation 13:8). Before humanity ever existed, God
foresaw what our need would be. Redemption through the
blood of Christ was no accommodation on God's part to the un-
foreseen. Satan may be powerful, but he can never take God
by surprise. Whatever temptations he brings us are already
known to God who rules over all. Ours is an enduring salvation;
in the eternal purpose of the Almighty, it brings everlasting life
to everyone who trusts in Christ. Oh, the wonder of the redemption God has provided for us through "the Lamb slain from the
foundation of the world"!

DECEMBER 10

*Praise be to the God and Father of our Lord Jesus Christ,
who has blessed us in the heavenly realms with every
spiritual blessing in Christ* (EPHESIANS 1:3, NIV).

Where are you living your Christian life? "Why," you reply,
"I'm living it at home, at work, in the town or city where I
dwell." Your answer is quite correct, so far as it goes. But it
relates to only one aspect of your Christian life. For every Christian leads a twofold life—his outward life and his inner one,
which Paul describes in Colossians as the life that "is hid with
Christ in God" (Colossians 3:3). The outward life has its
earthly location; the inner life has a higher environment. Its
sphere, as Paul shows us in this beautiful doxology, is "in the
heavenly realms." This is language the world cannot understand; of all the epistles Ephesians is for the unregenerate the
most incomprehensible. Yet we who are in Christ know, if now
only in part, that our inner life reaches to "heavenly realms,
with every spiritual blessing in Christ."

DECEMBER 11

The Lord spoke unto Moses: If a person sins by unfaithfulness to the Lord and he lies to his neighbor about storage, or a deposit, or a robbery, or an extortion . . . he must restore what he robbed . . . and add one-fifth of its value to it (LEVITICUS 6:1-5, Berkeley).

In addition to the sacrifice of a ram without blemish, the trespass-offering required returning the whole amount of which the neighbor had been defrauded plus one-fifth. The practice of restitution is too frequently forgotten today. But should we, who are not under the law but under grace, be any less generous in righting wrongs than were the Jews? Christian restitution applies to more than money and property; it also concerns the far more precious realm of personhood. Wounding another's feelings, attacking his reputation, needlessly disturbing his peace of mind—these require the forgiveness of Christ. And they also demand restitution through sincere contrition and humble apology, cost our pride what this may.

DECEMBER 12

Philip saith unto him, Come and see (JOHN 1:46b).

The Gospels tell us comparatively little about Philip. But they do make clear that he knew how to lead people to Christ. To Nathanael he said, "Come and see." And when certain Greeks in Jerusalem wanted to see Jesus they turned to Philip for help (John 12:20, 21).

We are not told that Philip was learned or eloquent, or specially gifted in any way. But there was one thing he did know, and that was how to invite men to come to Christ. He was a true evangelist, because he gave the Gospel invitation. "Come" was Philip's word, and he doubtless used it often.

To preach a great sermon demands eloquence. To write a great book requires literary genius. But to say "Come" to those who are unsaved is within the ability of each one of us. It is something any Christian can do.

Do you say "Come"? Do you invite people to church and to other places where they will hear the Gospel? Above all, do you invite them to come to Christ Himself?

DECEMBER 13

It was impossible for God to lie (HEBREWS 6:18).

There is one thing God cannot do. It is entirely out of the question for the Almighty ever to violate His nature. Sin is contrary to His nature, and lying is sin. Therefore, we have the assurance of this great axiom, "It is impossible for God to lie," or as Dean Alford translated it, "It is impossible for God ever to lie."

Christian friend, cling to this declaration, rest your life upon it. Meditate on it, and realize that it guarantees the integrity of every single promise in the Bible. For the Bible is God's Word, and He can never lie. Why, the God who inspired the Holy Scriptures undergirds their trustworthiness by the very integrity of His nature!

> *How firm a foundation, ye saints of the Lord,*
> *Is laid for your faith in his excellent Word!*

DECEMBER 14

Answer, you rulers: are your judgments just? . . . Never! Your hearts devise all kinds of wickedness (PSALM 58:2, NEB).

"Your hearts devise all kinds of wickedness." Though initially addressed to unjust rulers, these words have a more general application. They show us the hidden springs of evil, the secret source of wrong, within mankind. To be sure, our words, hands, and deeds are the instruments by which wickedness is done. But before it ever finds outward expression, it has been in our hearts. Within us, in our unregenerate desires, iniquity is born. All the evil in the world has come out of the human heart.

How this fact drives us to the cross! How it shows even the best of us that we must be cleansed in the inmost recesses of our being. And this is what Christ does for all who trust in Him. His precious blood, shed for us on the cross, cleanses us from all sin. In Him we have the renewing of our minds, and from His Spirit, who dwells in our hearts by faith, comes everything that honors God and helps our fellow man

DECEMBER 15

Iron sharpeneth iron; so a man sharpeneth the countenance of his friend (PROVERBS 27:17).

Notice that the figure itself has to do with things that are similar; it is not iron and lead, nor iron and tin, but iron that is opposed to iron. Friends, like husbands or wives, must be matched. And if true marriages are made in heaven, so are true friendships. As a wise man said, Christian friendship is a matter of divine election. Thank the Lord for your friends. They are one of the provisions for your growth in favor with God and man.

DECEMBER 16

Thy righteousness is like the mountains of God (PSALM 36:6, RSV).

It is a valid criticism of the modern mind that it has well nigh forgotten the righteousness of God. God is merciful and faithful. God is love. But He is also holy and just. What a magnificent metaphor David used! It brings to our imagination the great mountains reaching to the heavens in their snowclad majesty. Men build their towers and skyscrapers, yet they will never build a McKinley or an Everest.

But look again at the first element of the figure—God's righteousness. Other great religions recognize the incompatibility of man's sin and the divine righteousness, but other religions endeavor to reconcile the two by what man does. Christianity alone offers true reconciliation, because it shows us the full benefits of what God has done in giving His only Son to bring us, unrighteous and sinful though we are, to Himself. So the mountains of God stand as a sublime and enduring reminder of what God has done to make His righteousness available to us sinful men and women. The psalmist's metaphor is not merely for our admiration but for our response, because it points to "the righteousness of God which is by faith of Jesus Christ unto all and upon all them that believe" (Romans 3:22).

DECEMBER 17

For many walk, of whom I have told you often, and now tell you even weeping, that they are the enemies of the cross of Christ (PHILIPPIANS 3:18).

There are some who actually hate the saving work of Jesus Christ. It is of such that Paul is speaking in this verse. He is thinking of those who are so opposed to the atonement as to be justly called by the awful name of "enemies of the cross of Christ."

Do we find it easy to talk of them? Paul did not. In his mention of them here in Philippians, there are these significant words—"and now[I] tell you even weeping." The spectacle of such deliberate rejection of Christ touched Paul's heart. It moved him to tears, because he knew that enmity to the cross of Christ leads men to destruction. What about us? Do we love our Lord and our fellow men enough to be deeply stirred when we see those who, to their eternal loss, are despising the cross on which the Prince of glory died?

DECEMBER 18

But you shall receive power, when the Holy Spirit has come upon you: and you shall be my witnesses . . . (ACTS 1:8, NASB).

The Lord Jesus, after promising power through the Holy Spirit, said, "You shall be my witnesses." His promise was kept. At Pentecost the Holy Spirit came upon the waiting disciples. And ever since, He has come into the hearts of all who have believed in Christ. Therefore He is in your heart and in mine. But are we what our Lord said we should be? Are we really witnesses to Him?

Notice Jesus' exact words—"my witnesses." A weakness in Christian testimony into which even the most devoted of us may slip is that of being witnesses to ourselves more than to our Lord. But it is not our own experiences or our own thoughts, but only the Lord Jesus Himself, who must be at the center of Spirit-empowered Christian witness. To be sure, human life is the context of witnesses, and so we cannot avoid all references to our own experience. Nevertheless, we must always aim to make Christ so central that others will say, "What a wonderful Lord!" rather than, "What a remarkable person that was who spoke!"

DECEMBER 19

They profess that they know God; but in works they deny him (TITUS 1:16).

There are some things God has joined together, and among them are faith and works. God means them to be as inseparable as cause and effect. For any Christian to divorce them is perilous.

Though this verse from Titus applied specifically to certain people in the Cretan church, it also stands as a warning to all who sever religion from morality. The warning is universal in application because the danger is a continuing one, particularly for those of us who stress sound doctrine. There are many who would sooner die than deny their Lord in their words, yet with thoughtless unconcern they deny Him in their deeds. Were believers to give as much thought to their acts for Christ as they do to what they say about Him, the life of the Church would be greatly strengthened.

DECEMBER 20

He that hath the bride is the bridegroom: but the friend of the bridegroom, which standeth and heareth him, rejoiceth greatly because of the bridegroom's voice: this my joy therefore is fulfilled. He must increase, but I must decrease (JOHN 3:29, 30).

John the Baptist is speaking. He has just witnessed to Christ in answer to a question about baptism. This witness, as the first part of our text shows, he now puts in the form of a little parable. Christ, of course, is the bridegroom. John, likening himself to the friend of the bridegroom who delights even in the sound of the bridegroom's voice, says, "This my joy therefore is fulfilled." Then he utters a declaration of sublime self-effacement, "He must increase, but I must decrease." And this too is intimately related to the fulfillment of his joy. For John has found the source of true happiness. He has found it in the exaltation of his Lord.

How is it with us? Can we say that honoring Christ really rounds out our joy? Are we willing and even determined to decrease, so that Christ may be exalted?

DECEMBER 21

The heart is the most deceitful of all things, and desperately sick; who can fathom it? (JEREMIAH 17:9, NEB).

Who indeed can know the heart of man? Thank God there is One who can and does know it. Of Him we read in the second chapter of John's Gospel, "He knew all men, and needed not that any should testify of man: for he knew what was in man" (John 2:24). The Lord Jesus is the divine Physician. No one ever had insight like His, for He sees behind the actions into the thoughts and behind the thoughts into the secret motives of the heart. His penetrating gaze guarantees the perfection of His healing; no symptom of the sick soul escapes the accuracy of His diagnosis. And for all the deceitfulness and iniquity and desperate illness He sees, He has the sovereign remedy, even His own blood, which He shed for us.

We cannot even make a beginning in the Christian life without being willing to say from the bottom of our hearts such words of confession as these: "There is no health in us." The man who knows he is sick calls the doctor; and only those who realize the desperate condition of their souls will turn to the great Physician, who takes us just as we are and heals us in His love.

DECEMBER 22

O Lord of hosts, blessed is the man that trusteth in thee (PSALM 84:12).

Other beatitudes are limited; this one is universal. Not everyone is poor in spirit, pure in heart, or meek. Yet despite his inadequacy, everyone may trust in the Lord and so have His blessing. For this Old Testament beatitude, which recurs elsewhere in the Psalms, is the ground and basis of all spiritual blessing. Let the proud trust in the Lord, and He will make them humble; let the impure set their belief on Him, and He will cleanse them; let the self-sufficient place their faith in God, and He will create in them a hunger and thirst after His righteousness. Spiritual blessing is available to everyone, but we must use the key to this blessing. That key is trust. There is no exception; everyone who would be blessed of God *must* trust in Him.

DECEMBER 23

And Mary said, My soul doth magnify the Lord, and my spirit hath rejoiced in God my Saviour (LUKE 1:46, 47).

The experience of Mary, the mother of our Lord, was unique. As the angel said, she was "blessed . . . among women" (v. 28). But her rejoicing at the impending birth of the Saviour also has an aspect common to all Christians. Every believer may echo Mary's word of praise. We, too, who know Christ as Saviour, may sing: "My soul doth magnify the Lord." We who know the meaning of Christmas, because we have received God's greatest Gift, may also say, "My spirit hath rejoiced in God my Saviour." For you and me Christ is none other than "God my Saviour." The child whom we think of with adoration was God manifest in the flesh. Called by His human name of Jesus, because He was to save His people from their sins, He was God. His mother knew this by the intuition of the Holy Spirit. And the same Spirit bears witness with our spirits as to who Jesus is. So let us come and adore Him, for He is Christ our Lord.

DECEMBER 24

Then said I, Lo, I come (in the volume of the book it is written of me,) to do thy will, O God (HEBREWS 10:7).

We should not dare to draw aside the veil from this scene, did not the Word of God itself do so. For here, quoted from Psalm 40:7, 8, is a reference to the conversation of the pre-existent Son with His Father that took place in eternity and led to our redemption. Sometimes in a bitter hour of despair and disillusionment a man may say, "I didn't ask to be born into the world." But there was One who did.

Today is Christmas eve. And it is Christmas eve only because the Son of God, who was equal with the Father in eternal glory, chose to be born into this world of sin and poverty, anguish and darkness. There never was a greater display of divine grace than was seen in the cradle at Bethlehem. For the child who lay there could have said were He to have spoken, "Lo, I come (in the volume of the book it is written of me,) to do thy will, O God." Knowing His gracious choice to take upon Himself our humanity, let us thank Him with all our hearts for becoming our Immanuel, our God with us, our Saviour and Our Lord.

DECEMBER 25

The grace of God has appeared, bringing salvation to all men (Titus 2:11, NASB).

This beautiful verse points to the supreme manifestation of God's grace in the Lord Jesus Christ. In Bethlehem a stupendous miracle took place. The child born in the stable and laid in the manger was at the same time the gracious God incarnate. He who nestled in His mother's arms was "our great God and Savior, Christ Jesus" (v. 13, NASB), the Lord of heaven and earth.

Why was He born? Why did this miracle of miracles take place? Our text explains why. He appeared, it says, "bringing salvation to all men." This is what Christmas is all about. As Matthew tells us, He was named "JESUS: for he shall save his people from their sins" (Matthew 1:21). Through Him salvation is available to everybody. So let us celebrate on this happiest of days the marvelous good news of our Saviour's birth. Let us celebrate it not only as the turning point of history, which it actually was, but as the present, living reality that it now is, because Christ dwells in every believing heart.

DECEMBER 26

In the beginning was the Word, and the Word was with God, and the Word was God (John 1:1).

Only an inspired pen could write this declaration. For here the veil is lifted, as John opens his Gospel with this majestic assertion of our Lord's eternal preexistence in equality and oneness with the Almighty.

The virgin birth, with which Matthew and Luke begin their respective Gospels, is a profound truth; but it was only the beginning of Christ's incarnation, not of His life. He whose human body was formed in Mary's womb was eternally preexistent in heavenly unity with the Father. Some would call these words of John merely an echo of Alexandrian philosophy. But they are infinitely more than that. They assure us of the unique validity of the prophetic name given our Lord before His birth (Isaiah 7:14; Matthew 1:22, 23). Not only was He named Immanuel, but in very truth He who in the beginning was with God and was God is our Immanuel, our "God with us."

DECEMBER 27

Can two walk together, except they be agreed? (AMOS (3:3).

Who are the two referred to in this verse? Ultimately they are God and man. "Enoch walked with God," says Genesis 5:24.

None of us can be an Enoch and remain in disagreement with God. The price of the godly life is conformity to the divine will. If the two, God and us, are to agree, it is always we who must conform to God and not God to us. There is only one way to agree with God and this is by faith. "By faith Enoch was translated that he should not see death," the author of Hebrews wrote (11:5). And so our hope for a daily walk with God and a joyful entrance into His presence rests upon faith in Christ, who came that we might be reconciled to God.

DECEMBER 28

We do not have a high priest who is unable to sympathize with our weaknesses, but we have one who has been tempted in every way, just as we are—yet was without sin (HEBREWS 4:15, NIV).

Much discussion has centered around the phrase, "without sin." Some have even assailed it as detracting from the comfort derived from belief in the humanity of our Lord. "For," they say, "if Christ never sinned, His temptation must be remote from us who are so prone to fall."

But the objection is wrong. Our Lord Jesus was indeed "tempted in every way, just as we are." Yet of all humanity, He, the Son of man, was completely without sin; He alone conquered every temptation that can assail our human nature. And that is the very reason why He is qualified to lead the way to victory over the sin that so easily besets us.

Imagine a man struggling with some fierce temptation. He has as counselor one who, having faced the identical temptation, has never yielded but, in the very heat of the struggle, has won the victory. That man is qualified to help, because he himself has won the battle. So it is with our Lord. There is no temptation known to man that He has not gloriously overcome in our behalf.

DECEMBER 29

Let brotherly love continue (HEBREWS 13:1).

God has made certain spiritual graces especially attractive to non-Christians. Among these is brotherly love. The life that reflects it is a winsome life. The church in which it prevails has a compelling testimony that powerfully compliments the witness of its pulpit.

Brotherly love is more than mere benevolence. It is characterized by deep concern for the total welfare of others. It springs from a regenerated heart that is filled with the love of Christ. None of us Christians can afford to forget that, no matter what our circumstances may be, we must continue to manifest brotherly love.

DECEMBER 30

And I saw a new heaven and a new earth: for the first heaven and the first earth were passed away; and there was no more sea. And I John saw the holy city, new Jerusalem, coming down from God out of heaven, prepared as a bride adorned for her husband (REVELATION 21:1,2).

The two closing chapters of Revelation are the altogether glorious finale of the written Word. The battle is over. Satan is dealt with, sin judged, divine justice vindicated. Wonderfully beautiful and shining with heavenly glory are these pages. By all means take time today to read them slowly and prayerfully.

The Bible is a very old book, but it speaks more authentically of the future than the newest publications. The Bible deals fully and honestly with sin; it sets forth the only accurate picture of God's judgment of evil. Yet it is also the most optimistic of books. What a future it portrays in these final chapters! Beginning with the appearance of "a new heaven and a new earth" and "the holy city, new Jerusalem, coming down from God out of heaven, prepared as a bride adorned for her husband," they are suffused with the light of eternity itself. Reading them, who can doubt the blessings that our God has in store for His people. Truly, "Eye hath not seen, nor ear heard, neither have entered into the heart of man, the things which God hath prepared for them that love him" (1 Corinthians 2:9).

DECEMBER 31

You shall remember all the way which the Lord your God has led you (DEUTERONOMY 8:2, RSV). . . . *Forgetting those things which are behind, and reaching forth unto those things which are before, I press toward the mark for the prize of the high calling of God in Christ Jesus* (PHILIPPIANS 3:13, 14).

"Remember" . . . "forgetting." These words, while in contrast, are complementary, not contradictory.

Just as Moses enjoined the Israelites, who were about to enter the promised land, to remember all the way the Lord had led them during their wanderings in the wilderness, so we who stand on the threshold of another year should remember the many ways in which the Lord has led us during the past twelve months. We may not understand why some testings and difficulties have been in our path any more than we may claim credit for the blessings the Lord has brought us. But every Christian, thinking back over the past year, should acknowledge with thanksgiving that, whether or not he has realized it, the Lord has truly been with him.

Forgetting those things which are behind . . . I press toward the mark for the prize of the high calling of God in Christ Jesus." Here Paul gives us the obverse truth. For the turn of the year is like a door that opens from the long corridors of the past onto the hopeful vistas of the future. What were the things Paul insisted on forgetting? Not the blessings of the Lord and His former leadings—Paul's writings are too full of thanksgiving for that—but rather the things that in self-righteousness he had once relied upon (vv. 4-6). Turning his back on these, he strove with all his might to reach the goal of "the high calling of God in Christ Jesus."

So as the year closes, let us take time in grateful prayer to remember how the Lord has led us, and then, looking unto Him who is both our divine Guide and our glorious goal, recommit ourselves to His service in the year ahead.

> *Awake, my soul, stretch every nerve,*
> *And press with vigor on;*
> *A heav'nly race demands thy zeal,*
> *And an immortal crown.*

FOR SPECIAL TIMES

GOOD FRIDAY

And sitting down they watched him there (MATTHEW 27:36).

These Roman soldiers watched the crucifixion as just one more of the brutal spectacles they had become hardened to. But all the time they had their own personal share in it. For the event which they saw and which we commemorate on Good Friday is related to every human life. There are many who, like the Roman soldiers, think they can look on Calvary impersonally and impassively. But they are wrong. Sin nailed Jesus Christ to the cross, and our common sinfulness links every one of us to Calvary.

But there is another link. It is that of faith. All who turn from an impersonal attitude of unconcern, and see on the cross their Saviour dying for them, are bound to the atonement with the cords of His redeeming love. On the other hand, this is also true: no one who looks on Christ's death as only an historical event or a religious spectacle can really be a Christian. Observing the cross merely as a spectacle does not save anyone. But when we believe that we are identified with what happened there and that Christ died for us, then we become new persons in Him. As you look back to the suffering Saviour on this Good Friday, are you saying of Him, "the Son of God who loved me and gave himself for me" (Galatians 2:20, RSV)?

EASTER

Believest thou this? (JOHN 11:26).

This is the great triumphant day of the Church. It is a day for affirmation, not for argument, because it commemorates the tremendous event when Christ broke the bonds of death and in His glorified body rose from the grave.

Said the Lord Jesus to Martha, as He was about to raise her brother Lazarus, who had been dead for days, "I am the resurrection, and the life: he that believeth in me, though he were dead, yet shall he live: and whosoever liveth and believeth in me shall never die" (John 11:25). Then He asked her the all-important question, "Do you believe this?" That was before He Himself had conquered death by rising from the grave. And Martha made full confession of her belief in Christ as the resurrection and the life.

You and I are looking back this Easter day through the centuries to the glorious climax of our Lord's ministry. Yet to us also there comes the same question, "Do you believe this?" Nothing short of an affirmative answer, signifying full and wholehearted trust in the risen Christ, will suffice. In the face of the mighty resurrection of our Saviour, neither conjecture, supposition, nor rationalization will do. It is not enough to suppose, or think, or even hope, that Christ actually rose from the dead. God is asking for our full trust in His divine Son, who is our everliving Lord. "If thou shalt confess with thy mouth the Lord Jesus, and shalt believe in thine heart that God hath raised him from the dead, thou shalt be saved" (Romans 10:9).

IN THE TIME OF TROUBLE

But Jesus immediately said to them: "Take courage! It is I. Don't be afraid" (MATTHEW 14:27, NIV).

There was a storm on Galilee. The frightened disciples saw Jesus walking on the water. To their terrified cries He responded, "Take courage! It is I. Don't be afraid."

Here are three essentials for Christian living in times of trouble: (1) "Take courage!" When believers are in trouble, Jesus' first word to them is one of encouragement. No matter how severe the storms in our lives, He would have us take heart. (2) "It is I." Without this assurance, the call to courage would be a mockery. Storms are real, sorrows crushing, dangers menacing. Relying only on ourselves, we have nothing to be encouraged about. But when Jesus says, "It is I," then even in the darkest hours we can find strength and comfort, for He is our Immanuel, our "God with us." (3) "Don't be afraid." No matter what the extremity of our need, Jesus can deliver us from being intimidated by it. He still says, "Don't be afraid," and in our deepest distress we still have His words, "Let not your heart be troubled, neither let it be afraid." Nothing that can happen to a human being can ever shut Jesus out of a believer's life.

THANKSGIVING DAY

Praise ye the Lord (PSALM 148:1).

Thanksgiving Day reminds us of the obligation of everyone to be grateful to God. We look back and realize how much we owe the Heavenly Father. We are His creatures, the work of His hands. We owe Him thanks for His goodness each day. It is through His bounty that we have our daily bread; it is by His mercy that our lives are sustained. Every blessing comes from Him. So it is right and proper for all people everywhere to thank God, because all are recipients of His grace. "He makes his sun to rise on the evil and on the good, and sends rain on the just and on the unjust" (Matthew 5:45, RSV). Yes, Thanksgiving Day by its very nature should be a time of universal praise to God.

But for Christians, Thanksgiving is a very special celebration. For believers no time of prayer, least of all on this day, is complete without praising God. One of the oldest names for the central act of worship in which we remember our Lord's death till He comes is the "Eucharist," which means "thanksgiving." Confession and humiliation go with the Christian observance of Thanksgiving, as we think of the riches of God's grace and His great mercy in saving us.

INDEX